DATE DUE			
JAN 25 78			
JAN 24 79			
MAY 26 80			

POLICY AND ADMINISTRATION

POLICY
and
ADMINISTRATION

PAUL H. APPLEBY, *Dean of the*
Maxwell Graduate School, Syracuse University

UNIVERSITY OF ALABAMA PRESS, UNIVERSITY, ALA.

To Ruth

Preface

A PROMISE, given perhaps too casually at a meeting of the American Society for Public Administration, to deliver a series of lectures at the University of Alabama, has resulted in this book. It has had to be written in bits and at odd moments, and no doubt suffers also from an attempt to make both a book and a series of addresses. It is an effort to express appreciation of the distinguished program going forward at the University of Alabama under the direction of Professor Roscoe C. Martin.

The attempt here is to sketch something like a full-dimensional picture of public administration and thus to indicate its great, although subordinate, significance. The picture is not intended in any sense to be a defense of government, although it will often have that appearance. Rather, the purpose is to assert that government, particularly executive government, generally resembles this picture. Many questions involving degrees to which and places at which the descriptions apply and concerning possibilities for improvements in governance should be suggested by the picture, but I believe they will be questions more relevant to reality than many others commonly raised.

Acknowledgment is made to *Social Action* for permission to reprint in slightly rewritten form the concluding paper.

P. H. A.

Contents

Fallacies and Definitions

THE MAKERS of the American Constitution built it in some respects on the basis of erroneous descriptions—such as Montesquieu's—of the British system. This in particular is the origin of the formal separation of powers which, however qualified in the Constitution or in practice, is a central feature of American governmental structure.

1

Constitutional separation of powers in turn has influenced tremendously the development of political thought in this country, as of course it has influenced practice. The effort of theory has been in considerable part to justify, to make real, to enlarge and to enforce the Constitutional pattern. This effort, in turn, has been supported by some of the necessities of the methods of scholarship. The human mind, when it works in a systematic or scientific manner, divides reality into parts for intensive study. The process puts a premium on definitions and distinctions. The division of labor among thinkers becomes itself a kind of separation of powers. Each academic discipline to a degree divorces itself from all others, and separates itself from consideration of the whole reality. Each method used by each discipline is capable of producing insights— but partial and specialized insights. The mind thus abstracts from reality various shadows of parts of reality, and finds itself able to do many things with these shadows which it could not do with the total reality. But these shadows may contribute to misunderstanding, as they may contribute to understanding. Certainly, as the fruits of analysis multiply, the task of synthesis becomes more and more difficult and challenging.

At all events, students of government found the Constitutional separation of powers congenial to their own needs to define and to divide into parts for special study the whole of our governmental reality. And certainly it is possible and useful to identify certain types of actions as "legislative," others as "executive," and others as "judicial." Certainly it is possible and useful to consider "policy" apart from "administration," to distinguish between "policy" and "politics," and between "municipal government," "county government," "state government" and "federal government." Similarly, there are useful distinctions between Washington and field, between national and regional, between one administrative level and another, between economic policy and welfare policy—and many others.

Most scholarly efforts in the field of government (curiously similar to pressure-group efforts) were long, and quite naturally, attempts to look at government from single, separate vantage points on the basis of certain simplifying assumptions. For a half-century or so while political science was developing as a distinct discipline, much of its literature tended to accept as substantially real a separation of powers which excluded from administration any—or at least any important—policy-making functions. Under such a theory of separation, a civil service system was justified, accepted, and probably to a small extent over-sold.

The President was recognized as an outstanding exception, but the President's office was conceived of in personal rather than institutional terms. He was a policy-maker as an individual and as President, not as Chief Executive. He occupied a level not merely a long step higher than his Cabinet but almost in another world.

Other exceptions were noted and struggled with, both by political scientists and by politicians. Some positions, altogether not making any very clear pattern, were recognized as policy-making and therefore subject to Senatorial confirmation. In professional circles, efforts were made to distinguish between "administrative" and "executive," some elevating the first term, others the second. But generally it was long believed that administrative personnel were not policy-making. This was at a time when the executive government did not differ markedly in nature from its successor segments of the government of today.

In the meantime, however, the government has gone on, developing in some parts under restraint of prevailing theory, in some parts in disregard of theory, in all parts reflecting governmental efforts to survive under changing conditions.

Sir Cecil Carr gives examples of this process of adjustment in his book, *Concerning British Administrative Law*. He quotes Maitland as observing that the medieval criminal law could be preserved because a Court of Star Chamber would supply its deficiencies; the old private law could be preserved because the Court of Chancery was composing an appendix to it; trial by jury could be preserved, developed and transfigured because other modes of trial were limiting it to an appropriate sphere. Carr then goes on to say:

Will the historian some day go further and say that our old-fashioned national law, unable out of its own resources to meet the requirements of a new age, has been preserved because it was supplemented by a system, however unsystematic, of administrative tribunals?

The preservation and development under changing conditions of adequate facilities for governance harmonious with democratic values is the first concern of both students and practitioners in the field of government. The extent to which and the ways in which separations of power exist in fact or should exist is a subordinate question. It is intended in these papers to explore one part of that question.

A clearer understanding of the present reality with respect to policy-making and administration is needed by many political scientists and by many students and practitioners of public administration. It is needed by newspaper correspondents who report on "bureaucracy" and government in general. It is badly needed by members of Congress suffering from a sense of inadequacy before extravagant popular expectations that Congress will function as *the* policy-making branch, and that individual members of Congress will be able to control specific administrative actions. They need better to understand their own actual practice, and to make it more consciously and thoughtfully a movement of role upward in levels of importance. Most of all, a clearer understanding is needed by citizens, confused by the complexity of government in complex society; they need to know how to fix responsibility, how to protect popular government, how to make democratic, citizen concerns central to that government.

2

It is widely believed that Congress has an exclusive responsibility for policy-making. Yet it is also

widely believed that policy is freely made by every
government official.   Many citizens also have accepted Justice Field's distinction between judicial
and legislative acts ("The one determines what the
law is, and what the rights of parties are with reference to transactions already had; the other pre-
scribes what the law shall be in future cases arising
under it.") and have observed all three branches of
the government performing both of the functions he
described.   Without extensively exploring the rami-
fications of all three branches, these papers will consider ways in which policy is made in the course of
administration.

In normal fashion the discussion would begin
with some definitions.   But definition in social
science is generally difficult, and often the source
of the misunderstanding one seeks to reduce.   Definition is particularly difficult when it has to do with
living, complex processes; when achieved, it is often
so broad as to have little meaning.   The attempt
here is to describe.

Both courts and administrators find in law things
Congress or legislatures had never consciously put
there.   In other cases, both resolve difficulties Congress or legislature had consciously left for them to
resolve.

Congress and legislatures make policy for the future, but have no monopoly on that function, as the
courts have no monopoly on the determination of

what the law is. Administrators are continually laying down rules for the future, and administrators are continually determining what the law is, what it means in terms of action, what the rights of parties are with respect both to transactions in process and transactions in prospect. Administrators make thousands of such decisions to one made by the courts. They act with regard for what the courts have decided and would be likely to decide, of course, but in considerable degree the power of the courts over administration is a reserve power. The power of legislative bodies is in a considerable degree, also, a reserve power over administration.

Administrators also participate in another way in the making of policy for the future; they formulate recommendations for legislation, and this is a part of the function of policy-making, even that policy-making which can be done fully only at the legislative level. Both administrative change and legislative change grow out of the popular scene, grow out of reactions to conditions as they have developed, reactions to what has been legislated, to what is being administered and the way it is being administered. Citizen reactions flow to the legislative body directly, and through the executive branch, and both currents are essential to the final product. As the current of citizen reaction moves through the executive branch, it is given a certain organization. It gains also contributions growing out of administrative and expert considerations. The two currents from the people equip the legislature more fully than would the direct people-to-legislature current alone. In channeling one of the currents, the executive branch participates in policy-making.

It might be said, then, that legislative bodies make very general policy, and that administrators make policy by applying that general policy at successively less abstract levels. While there is truth in this, it is by no means uniformly valid. Claims bills regularly enacted in considerable number provide one familiar example of quite specific policy-making by Congress. Small claims of the same sort are settled administratively; the power of Congress with respect to claims is reserved not for the generally significant but for the large. Eliminations of specific appropriations for single jobs provide another kind of example. One may recall, too, the Congressional spanking given to a recent Secretary of the Treasury for changing the pay of charwomen in the Treasury building without specific Congressional approval.

On the other hand, many very broad policy decisions have been made within the executive branch. This is particularly true with respect to foreign policy, conduct of war, and public welfare. In New York State the Governor has great responsibility for very broad policy-making and legislative leadership.

The injection of Congress, or Congressional instrumentalities, into the "administrative" field further confuses the matter in the national government. Individual members of Congress, chairmen of committees, sub-committees and committees—none of which is "the Congress"—exercise a great deal of influence over, and sometimes actually exercise a direct control over, many matters that are commonly thought of as strictly administrative. Senator Smoot was an able example, and Congressman Andrew May was a venal example. The General Accounting Office is a Congressional creature, with executive control functions of so pervasive a sort as to be thought by many students of government to make the arrangement unconstitutional. The Government Printing Office is under the direct control of Congress, and as such it exercises a certain executive function, as well as being an indispensable service agency of the executive. In connection with the effectuation of the Administrative Procedures Act a few years ago the Printing Office made important policy decisions about what departmental procedures would be printed. The Congressional Committee on Printing makes quite specific administrative decisions. Joint Congressional-Executive commissions long have decided specifically the tracts to be purchased for wild life refuges and national forest additions. The Appropriations Committee has required notification of executive determinations with respect to locations and sizes of government hospitals, the inference being that the committee would veto decisions they did not like.

3

If one wishes, then, to define policy as that which Congress decides, and administration as that which the executive branch does, policy and administration may be regarded as separated, and the definitions, like so many others having to do with social processes, become rather meaningless. Similarly, within the executive branch, if policy is defined as decision-making at top levels and administration is decision-making and decision-application at lower levels, a kind of separation is achieved, but the definitions are not useful.

The position taken in this discussion is that description is more appropriate than definition; that many types of decisions involving policy-making are and must be delegated as a usual thing; that, on the other hand, almost any type of decision may become on occasion a matter for top-level consideration and determination, even for popular determination; that the movement of work materials and decisions perpendicularly and laterally in the levels and divisions of government is of the essence of both policy-making and administration; and that the whole governmental context is important to legislation, to administration, to policy-making, and to court decisions. By "context" it is intended to suggest that courts can be judged and their decision-making understood only in the light of what is done by Congress and by administrators; that administration can be judged and its policy-making understood only in the light of what is done by courts and Congress and the administrative hierarchy itself; that Congressional policy-making similarly can be understood only in the light of what is done by courts and by administrators; that the three branches can be understood only in the light of popular political activities.

The position here taken is also that exercise of discretion in decision making is everywhere in the government of the same nature, but of many orders, and that the order of a particular decision is always subject to final determination in a great political complex of pressure and agitation present or prospective in which felt need, history and precedent work through various interlocking governmental institutions, each distinguished by preponderant but not exclusive responsibilities. Constitutional structure and principle and law provide much of the history, precedent and institutional pattern. Public sense of need and the institutions of government are in this aspect alike, and together are dynamic factors working through political means to effect ever new adjustment to an ever changing social whole. The institutions are flexible and dynamic in considerable part because of their political nature, their political environment and their political responsibility; politics brings felt need and governmental institutions into whatever harmony is achieved.

The great distinction between government and other organized undertakings is to be found in the wholly political character of government. The great distinction between public administration and other administration is likewise to be found in the political character of public administration. Policy-making in private business may take place with reasonable public safety at many levels because it is influenced by supply and demand, by competition and by an intra-organizational play of diverse interests. Policy-making may take place with reasonable public safety at many levels in the executive government because the order of any decision is always *subject to* political determination, and arrived at in a political environment. This is to say that by political agitation any decision normally or administratively treated as of a low order of importance and delegated to a low hierarchal level of responsibility may be called up for higher-level consideration.

Subject to such calling up, normal administrative or legislative fixing of the order of a particular decision—the level at which it may be made—is done by a subtle process of political evaluation. That evaluation is reached generally through anticipation of popular reaction; as a response to experience, convention and precedent; under pressure from interests directly concerned; under pressures from other parts of the government; and in specific cases through popular debate, campaigns and elections. The order of a particular decision is preliminarily and tentatively determined within the executive branch by political, administrative, procedural, technical or factual and social evaluations. These evaluations constitute a more or less rough consensus of the horizontally and perpendicularly associated individuals and groups participating in the institutional and environmental context. The level at which a decision is to be made, therefore, may be shifted downward or upward as evaluations point to more or less controversy, or to more or less "importance." Importance within the administrative organization turns in some part on expert valuations; in some degree on novelty; in some part on prerogatives and other institutional valuations; in some part on dimensions and scope of the action—the weight of impact it will have or has had on citizens, and the number of citizens affected; in some part on ideal values, such as are involved, for example, in questions of the *kind* of impact on even a single citizen. In very considerable part all this is reaction to diverse political forces.

It is a process, then, in which many unlike things are weighed on the same scales, and simultaneously. It is like, but much more complicated than, the process of economic evaluation in which investment and consumption goods through popular processes of supply and demand, and through competition and administration are weighed on dollar scales to determine relative values of a bottle of Lydia Pinkham's Vegetable Compound, a quart of milk, a shirt, and the Empire State Building. In the field of economics, even the critics of laissez-faire are reluctant to rely heavily on a more rational or scientific scale. In the field of government, every kind and conception of value weighs on the political scale, and only political processes produce a reading. Public administration must contribute to the weighing, and to do that means to function politically.

Judgments of values in the course of administration are all theoretically—and any one judgment is in fact—subject to appeal to higher levels. The process of appeal usually is treated in restricted and legalistic terms, but it has a great and pervasive importance in the whole formal and informal operation of administrative business. Not merely the *nature* of citizen attitudes is weighed, but also the *intensity* of citizen feeling in the context of the whole social scene of the moment. Persistence of complaint, persistence of expressions of need, weighs heavily in political scales; but it weighs always in relation to other needs, hopes, complaints also on the scale, and their persistence. The reading of the scale changes constantly, and marked changes in reading send upward or downward in governmental levels the business to be decided.

4

An intricate process is subject to definition, but the definition must be made in such general terms as to reveal very little. Here administration is viewed as the government in direct action on behalf of and in restraint of citizens; policy-making in administration is the exercise of discretion with respect to such action. There are different orders of action, and different orders of policy, but these orders together are a continuum, with the fundamental common character which use of that term requires. Confusion enters when the continuum is denied. Wisdom comes when the process of decision-making is considered as a whole.

Actually, the earlier professional belief in the separation of policy and administration was never so clear, consistent or hard-and-fast as often has been assumed. The Constitution itself made no such complete separation. On the contrary, its provisions for a Presidential veto, for Presidential recommendations for legislation, and Presidential dominance in foreign and military policy injected the executive branch far into the policy-making field. Presidential responsibility of necessity was shared from the very beginning with the executive branch at large. White's administrative history, *The Fed-*

eralists, shows well begun in the first two administrations most of the kinds of policy-making now recognizable. If Hamilton, rather than Washington, exercised much of the policy leadership where Congress was concerned, it made the beginning more, not less, a foreshadowing of the general development.

Recognizing these Constitutional and historical facts and something of the actualities of practice, Goodnow's early discussion drew a line less abrupt between policy and administration than some who later quoted him seemed to know. Subsequently, many political scientists have noted the intermingling of policy-making and administration. Gulick as far back as 1933 positively denied their separation.

Louis Brownlow, a pioneer in the field of city managership, admitted years later that when he was a city manager he was an "important political figure." In a similar way, Professor Merriam in a series of lectures at Syracuse University in 1947 declared that "the executive has become fully as political as the legislature" and referred to policy-making and administration as a "circular process."

Thus, the long attempts to make sharp and real the separation of powers, the separations of policy-making and administration and politics and administration, have been undergoing abandonment. Perhaps the most stubborn withdrawal from their former ground is being made by lawyers. In their shift they are principal protagonists of an effort to secure a separation of powers within the executive branch as an extension of earlier thinking.

Another dichotomy, familiar to philosophy and to social science generally, has recently been presented as having special significance within the administrative process. Professor Simon in his book, *Administrative Behavior*, has attempted to illuminate administration by drawing a sharp distinction between fact-finding by administrators and their exercise of value-judgments. This appears as a sort of reincarnation of the early search for a line between policy-making and administration. It can be used to support other less thoughtful attempts at simplification in which the principal tool is a cleaver. Simon himself entered serious qualifications to the usefulness of the concept or even denied the reality of a dichotomy, for he admitted that facts at various levels are "intermediate values," and conceded that some "facts" are "controversial." Relevant to our present discussion, the significance of his book is in his recognition that value-judgment, hence policy-making, takes place in the administrative process.

Professor Reeves in casual discussions uses a diagram, about the source of which he is uncertain, portraying an intermingling of policy-making and execution and differentiating such interminglings according to hierarchal levels. The diagram pictures all policy-making and execution in an upright rectangle bisected by a kind of stairway running from a point near the upper right-hand corner to a point near the lower left-hand corner. The left half of the rectangle is designated as the area of policy-making, the other half the area of execution. According to this diagram, top executives occupy large policy areas and very small execution areas, while employees at the bottom of the hierarchy occupy very small policy areas and very large areas of execution.

This diagram has the values and the limitations Reeves attributes to it. It makes no allowance for a wide middle ground where policy and administration meet and mingle. It does not depict the reality of policy stimulation moving upward in the hierarchy whereby much policy apparently made at high levels actually develops out of lower levels. Similarly, it does not depict the reality of top-level execution determinations and stimulations penetrating into lower levels. Since the picture is two-dimensional, it does not permit adequate account of the effect of numbers in lower-level positions and of the absence of numbers in higher-level positions. A million employees, each having limited policy-making functions, together occupy more policy-making area than such a diagram suggests. Stereoscopic, motion-picture flow charts would more fully depict administrative reality. But the point is that this diagram, like so many other formulations attempted in re-

cent years, reflects growing recognition of the un-
reality of earlier efforts.

Executives do not sit at two different desks, treat-
ing policy at one and administration at the other.
Even intellectually, they more often deal with whole
problems than they deal with them as exclusively
problems of policy or problems of administration.

A detailed analysis of jobs at each hierarchal level
would show, it is believed, the same close relationships between policy-making and policy execution
at each level of the administrative hierarchy. It is
believed that the relationship exists even at the
Congressional level. The debates, legislative proposals and actual legislative provisions governing
the European Recovery Program provided a dramatic example; the debate and the legislation had
about as much to do with administrative determinations as with program policy. A cabinet member
similarly considers what to do and how to do it as
one problem; his instructions about program goals
have to be tied closely to, and are limited by, administrative directions designed to insure attain-
ment of the goals. The reports he listens to or reads
are both administrative reports and program reports
of achievement, shortcomings and difficulties. He
receives administrative and policy recommendations
alike. Some may be more strictly administrative,
some more strictly pertaining to policy, but without
program considerations there is no sense at all in

administration, and without administration nothing would happen with respect to policy. The functions of policy-making can not actually be vested exclusively at any one point or level in the government. Wherever there is action affecting the public, there is policy-making. Policy is made by means of all the political processes by which government is carried on. The various processes interact. Because the processes are varied, and because they do interact, the parts of the government are not isolated, autonomous or uncontrollable. Wherever the conduct of public affairs is not "taken out of politics," public control is possible; issues of administration as well as many others can be brought up for whatever consideration may be desired. Much administration may normally be left to administrators if all administration is a part of and subject to the various political processes. To this extent a rough, popular separation between policy and administration is valid.

It is not truly a separation, however; it is a kind of tentative delegation of power under which the public says, "We can not and will not bother with such matters as a general rule; we can attend well to only so much. But whenever we are much disturbed about something we are delegating to you, we shall suspend the delegation." Congress, the President, the head of a Department, the head of a Bureau, the head of a Division and the head of a

Section take similar positions, regularly exercising only those powers felt to be necessary to their respective general responsibilities, delegating everything else, and reserving the right to review anything done under delegation.

It is where administrative questions become policy questions of a sort needing public debate that the two merge at the public level. They merge at every governmental level in precisely the same way. This is to say that certain aspects of administration and certain aspects of policy require treatment together at the level of Congress; certain aspects of administration and policy must be treated together at the level of the President; certain aspects of both must be treated at the level of a Department head— and so on down the administrative hierarchy. At every level, the answer to the question "What is my judgment about this which I have to decide, or about this on which I need to have a judgment?" is a policy question. In the perspective of each successive level everything decided at that level and above is "policy," and everything that may be left to a lower level is "administration." In the perspective of an outside observer, policy and administration are treated together at every level.

Top executives in their policy-making roles are as dependent upon lower executives as the lower executives are dependent on higher ones. It is a reciprocal process from a strictly policy-making standpoint, and the processes of administration and policy-making are reciprocal. The movement of administrative materials up and down a hierarchy and across on various levels of associated hierarchies is the reality by which administration and policy-making take place concurrently.

5

Practitioners of public administration, too busy for and temperamentally disinclined to make systematic formulations of their learning, have been forced to a keener realization of the reality by a rapid succession of marked shifts in national policy. They are universally conscious of policy-making. Their deep involvement in policy has been demonstrated by enormous shifts in assignments and rank and by heavy job mortality for civil servants in key positions. Congress, long regarded as "the political branch" of the government, has had much more permanent tenure of key figures than have the civil service rolls of the executive departments, even without allowing for the far greater number of key civil service positions. Discarding of old policies and the development of new ones in the shifts from Hoover to Roosevelt to Truman, from 1928 boom to depression, to war, to reconversion, to post-war boom, to and from an opposition-dominated Congress were accompanied by rises and falls in favor of particular civil servants, and decapitation for many.

The resulting panic of the civil servants requires attention. To some extent panic develops because civil servants had expected more placid security than recurring needs for governmental adjustment can permit. To some extent lack of job security may require more use of financial indemnities for termination of services or demotion. A flexible and responsive government is the basic objective. Where this objective reduces job security unduly, other substitute types of security may be provided. The proportion of public personnel eligible for indemnification would be relatively small in most cases.

If there is ground for public fear because of a recognition of a policy-making function resting with administrative personnel, that fear needs to be considered. But one word of comfort on this point may not be out of place even in an introductory survey of the problem. The most extreme exercises of policy-making by executives have been admittedly unconstitutional, illegal, or highly questionable actions by certain Chief Executives. The Louisiana Purchase by Jefferson and the Emancipation Proclamation by Lincoln are outstanding examples. Reassurance would seem to lie in the fact that no one of the actions most seriously questioned from constitutional or legal standpoints has been itself disapproved by the people at the time or in subsequent history. This would suggest that the political institutions as a whole and the political environment within which the government operates have been in fact fully protective of the spirit even when the letter has been ignored. If this is true of the most dramatic and extensive exercises of power, may not the ordinary, organized, reciprocal operations of government, hedged in by pressures of many kinds, checked by competing and complementary prerogatives, exposed to publicity and opposition attack, with responsibility fixed in political officers who can be got at—may not this government be viewed with more than a little confidence and pride, as well as with constant concern?

6

Finally, it is submitted that the intermingling of policy and administration in our government is not new. It is more visible because both policy and administration are more visible; both have to do with many more things. But the *way* in which the government operates is largely the way in which it has been operated from the beginning.

"Administration" here is treated, therefore, as a broad term involving policy-making as well as execution. It is so treated because it is felt that a great deal of policy-making is implicit in what the executive branch does, and that it is important to recognize this policy-making function. "Management" involves the same intermingling of policy-making and execution, but it is here assigned arbitrarily to a lower level and used to signify executive action with least policy-making significance. Hence, public administration here becomes "that intermingling of policy-making and management which occurs below the levels of legislative, judicial, and popular-electoral policy determinations." Most presidential policy-making is on this level; a small part of it is on a level fully as elevated as the legislative and judicial levels. Some small part of the presidential policy-making power may be on a still higher level. But all of these levels are subordinate to the popular-electoral level.

CHAPTER II

The Eighth Political Process

ONE OF WEBSTER'S definitions of politics is this: "The science dealing with the organization, regulation and administration of a state, in both its internal and external affairs." The single word "politics" is invariably used in this sense in this discussion; in this sense politics is coextensive with government.

An official, an action, a function or an agency of government is viewed as "more political" or "less political" according to degree of involvement in the various processes characteristic of government, degree of subjection to popular control through elected officials and representatives, and degree of exposure to citizens. An official or agency in acting on behalf of the government is by that token political, but officials and agencies vary in the extent to which they partake of the whole governmental scene and its processes. Governments themselves vary in the same respects. Some live by and require more kinds of political processes than others; the

processes are more developed in some political societies than others; exposure of one government to
popular participating influence and control may be
much greater than that of another.   In this sense,
one government may be more political than another,
and in this sense there is always more of politics in
democratic government than in authoritarian government.   Partisan politics bears upon every aspect
of government, but for the most part rather generally and remotely; it is much less than the governmental whole.   Here we are attempting to consider
the whole governmental-political reality.

Here "more political" is a phrase generally con-
noting democratic virtue and responsibility.   It applies to situations, functions, agencies and officials
more controllable by and on behalf of the whole
public, less controllable by individuals or small,
special publics.

1

For purposes of this discussion, the government of
the United States will be considered as living by and
operating through eight distinct processes, all political processes.   It is contended that these processes,
like the parts of government, are not in fact sharply
separated but flow one into the other, the values of
each being dependent upon the values of the others
and the totality of their results.

The eight processes here discussed, therefore,

have principally illustrative validity. They provide us with a way of looking at the government. The government could be so regarded if the processes were arranged according to different schemes.

Although these processes have been modified and developed in the course of our national history, six of the eight have existed from the beginning, one came into being in the administration of Washington, and one more emerged with the Jackson administration. The numbers given to these categories are without significance, except that one existing from the time our government began is given the number eight for purposes of climax.

The first process on the list is the "Presidential Nominating Process." The existence of special machinery for nominating candidates for the Presidency has more political significance than usually is attributed to it. Before the time of Jackson this process was substantially a part of the legislative process; since then a separate line of obligation, appeal and determination has been maintained, and this has had far-reaching consequences. In the pre-Jackson period our government had a suggestion of parliamentary character, and since then we have developed something rather unique, often referred to as a "presidential system."

The second process in the list is the general nominating process. The methods of nominating candidates and the sizes of constituencies are far from uniform. Together they are an important feature of the scene, and for purposes of simplification all nominating procedures other than the Presidential are treated as one process.

The third process is voting—the electoral process. There are long ballots and short ballots, provisions for voting straight or mixed tickets, and differences in ways of voting, but the popular expression of choice among competing candidates is here regarded as a single, general process.

The fourth is the legislative process, involving everything that is done by legislative bodies, whether city councils, boards of supervisors in their ordinance-making role, state legislatures, or the national Congress.

The fifth is the judicial process.

The sixth is the party maintenance and operation process, exclusive of the making of nominations. This is a process not anticipated by the Constitutional fathers, but quickly developed with Hamilton and Jefferson as the first chief leaders of parties.

The seventh is the agitational process, involving the organization and political use of other than party groups, petitioning, public comment, debate and demands. This is a process in which independent voters and interest groups play a special role, influencing the parties to bid for their support, and consequently influencing all government.

The eighth is the administrative or executive process, involving everything done by agencies other than the legislative and judicial ones. This process is being especially considered here.

In terms of their significance to citizens, all of these processes have to be applied in and multiplied by the number of jurisdictions in which a particular citizen participates or by which he is affected, or multiplied by the total number of jurisdictions in the entire nation. The number of school boards, town or city councils, boards of supervisors, administrative jurisdictions, court districts or circuits, legislatures, the number of candidates, the number of party organizational units, the number of organizational units engaged in political agitation, the number of vehicles of expression—all these together give a rough measure of the political exposure of the various governmental entities and open possibilities of citizen participation in and influence on the processes of government.

It does not follow, of course, that the number of tickets, candidates, movements and jurisdictions is a measure of democracy or of usefulness to citizens. Short ballots, a consolidation of jurisdictions, and clarification of lines of responsibility in many instances are in the citizen's interest, reducing the confusion with which he has to deal, and enabling him more readily to arrive at judgments. What is an optimum set of citizen responsibilities and opportunities for participation in government is a question to which different answers must be given at different times and in varying situations. But whatever the answers may be, they will provide for a long time to come the eight general political processes that have been listed.

Through all of these processes in all of the jurisdictions, citizens influence or can influence the many parts of government which are together the whole government. The parts of government, influenced chiefly by certain citizens, in turn affect and are affected by other parts, which are more influenced by other citizens. The school board influences the council, the council influences the school board, both influence the board of supervisors, and the board of supervisors influences both of the others. The states influence the national government, the national government influences the states. The state departments of health, labor, welfare and agriculture influence their opposite numbers in the federal government, and vice versa. The various departments influence and are checked by each other.

The courts influence legislation, legislation influences the courts, courts and legislative bodies influence or control administrative agencies, and administrative agencies influence legislative bodies and courts. The appropriations committee influences other committees, and other committees influence the appropriations committee. All of the governmental entities are influenced in varying degrees (the variations will be discussed later) by citizen sentiment, by agitation, by the prospect of elections and by the actuality of elections already held, by what takes place in or what can take place in nominating procedures. In other words, all of these political organs influence each other and are themselves products of a political climate and political institutions. The purpose here is to explore in these terms the way in which policy-making in connection with administration takes place.

2

The degree of involvement of the various organs, agencies and officials engaged in governmental work in the eight political processes is by no means uniform. Variations in political involvement are a product of variation in these eight factors: (1) whether the officials concerned are popularly elected; (2) whether they are appointed by officials who are elected; (3) the degree of freedom in selection exercised by elected officials in appointing subordinate officials; (4) whether tenure is subject to or independent of changes in elective posts; (5) the ease of removability or transferability, of demotion and promotion; (6) whether officials are appointed by officials appointed and removable by elective officials; (7) the functional relationships with other agencies—the amount of exposure to and influence by other agencies to which the officials are subjected, and the degree to which these other agencies are more or less politically exposed and responsible; (8) and, finally, the degree to which a particular governmental activity directly affects and is exposed to large numbers of citizens.

The courts, except for those whose judges are popularly elected, are easily the least politically exposed and politically responsible of all the governmental organs and agencies. Those whose judges have life tenure are especially remote from political control. Politically appointed, their political derivation and the time in which they act may be far from harmonious; even in theory, the integration of courts with the rest of the government is designed to make for slow adjustment between past and present. Finally, the public directly and specifically affected by court proceedings is on the whole small. Courts, consequently, are least "pushed around" by the public and least subject to direct political control. Individual and small-group influence on courts is greatest at the local level, and least at the national level.

All legislative bodies except school boards, on the other hand, are generally subject to all or most of the eight political processes except the one involving Presidential nominations, and Congress is strongly affected by that one as well.

School boards in many jurisdictions and for long periods of time frequently operate in relative political vacuums, partly because of organic location, partly because of inadequate popular attention, partly because of a sentiment favorable to "the removal of schools from politics." In terms of hierarchal political control, school administration is usually fairly autonomous, by the same token, but in terms of dealing with patrons (factor 8 above) it has much political character. Usually, because of confused responsibilities with respect to revenues and other inter-organizational relationships (factor 7 above) the schools are less readily subject to integration with other aspects of government. But the schools are generally *subject to* popular political control whenever citizens become extraordinarily concerned about them.

The ways in which officials and organizations are politically involved, and the degrees of their involvement, are subject to wide variations within the executive departments and agencies.

The President, governors, mayors and county boards of supervisors are as completely involved in the political processes as are members of legislative bodies, the chief difference being that these officials usually are involved with and affected by larger constituencies, enabling or causing them individually to serve more fully as political synthesizers.

3

Executive departments and agencies may be usefully grouped, for the purposes of this examination, into eight categories.

In the first category may be placed the regulatory agencies often referred to as "quasi-judicial" or "quasi-legislative." The two terms may seem to suggest the existence of sharp differences in political character between two sub-groups, one having judicial remoteness and the other legislative-like involvement in political processes. Actually, the terms have little administrative significance. But because of procedures and conventions affecting all of these activities, for the whole regulatory category it is true that its political involvement is less than that or different from that of the executive government generally. This means that for this category political consideration and control in a wide sense are more likely than for other executive agencies to go over a long period of years from an extreme inattention to highly concentrated political attention.

A second category is represented by the Federal Reserve Board, which has only a quasi-governmental character. Members of the board are Presidentially appointed, according to a bi-partisan, interest-group, geographical formula, with long tenure, and with a system having district structure and an organic involvement with private banks. Of all the categories, it is least politically involved, least subject to complete popular control. Early proposals for Atomic Energy control, European recovery administration, and a Research Foundation would have established agencies falling into the same category. Some state agencies, some drainage and some reclamation districts have features of a similar sort. Some school boards may fall into this category.

A third category covers activities carried on through grants-in-aid, where inter-agency and intra-governmental associations are high (factor 7), but where control is diffused. States where the Agricultural Extension Service is controlled by associations of farmers, counties, state colleges and the United States Department of Agriculture provide an extreme example. The Extension Service in all states, the social security program, and many others fall into this category.

A fourth category is represented by the Farm Credit Administration, whereby the national government provides a tent loosely covering some 8,000 private or semi-private corporations, associated with regional organizations of quasi-governmental sort. In the relatively few instances where directors are appointed politically (governmentally) the appointments are subject to formulae and nominating procedures which magnify private or citizen-group control as contrasted with governmental control.

Organizations of the type of "government corporations" form the fifth category. They, like the regulatory commissions, are characteristically somewhat less subject to fully political and popular control, and are somewhat more subject to small-public pressures, because top responsibility is divided among the members of a board. They are also differentiated from typical executive agencies by being legally freed from a certain amount of normal political control, given an extra amount of discretion and flexibility. They are, on the whole, slightly more subject to political control by Congress than by the President, a little more than typical reliance being put on legislative changes, for policy adjustment, but the corporations are headed by appointed officials, usually subject to short terms and to removal. Corporations also are subject to some influence by other executive agencies, and many of their operations are widespread, open to and in contact with a large citizen public. They appear on the whole to be not as quickly responsive to policy changes, or to changes in conditions calling for policy changes, as regular government departments, because of their relative independence.

The sixth category is the one perhaps least justifying separate listing. It includes governmental institutions, such as prisons, asylums, orphanages and hospitals. These institutions are generally in fact subject to the same controls as other executive undertakings; they are listed separately simply because the practice is to give them little constant, general and public direction and attention. They are in fact relatively autonomous and exposed principally to small and underprivileged clienteles.

The seventh category includes a few agencies whose political control and exposure are rather especially limited to the chief executive and legislative branches, their activities being fairly sharply separated from the general social scene and not fully open to popular pressure. The State Department, dealing with matters outside our borders not directly encountered by most citizens except in the emergency of war, is a principal example. While foreign affairs are increasingly realized by citizens to have vast importance, the ability of the average citizen to get hold of and appraise relevant facts is extremely limited. The State Department has little direct contact with citizens, and citizens little direct association with the Department. The Department of Defense is another example. While on occasion it draws heavily on the public, its public relationships are most peculiar, and the defense organization is extraordinarily unequipped in a political way. Its political exposure is highly concentrated in the Chief Executive, Congress, and suppliers.

In considering this seventh category it must be noted that there is special justification for its relative political remoteness from detailed popular exposure and involvement. This justification applies particularly to the State Department and foreign policy. It is based on at least two distinguishing characteristics of the subject-matter involved. The first of these is that the greatest part of the political material of foreign policy exists outside our borders. The second is that it is developed and effectuated not so much in direct dealing with foreign publics as in direct dealing with sovereign governments.

Because of these characteristics, it is true that American citizens are less capable of knowing the content, and less representative of the total public values of foreign policy, than they are with respect to strictly domestic matters. Political control must always tend to be coextensive with political impact. Because foreign policy affects the rest of the world as well as the United States, foreign policy of the United States is properly only partially within the control of its citizens or even of their government.

Popular control of our foreign policy, therefore, is in the first instance influence rather than control, and is control only at the point where it becomes a veto over that part of foreign policy which is controllable by the government of the United States. In the nature of things, reliance on the leadership reposing in "the government" must be especially high in the case of foreign policy, and popular political influence on that policy must be to a considerable degree general influence of the whole political scene. Indirectly, such influence is very great. The State Department is a part of the government, and as such very much influenced by the rest of the government and the social scene generally. It is controlled by the President, chief partaker of the whole political scene. It is constantly influenced by and controllable by Congress, which as a body is similarly a partaker of the whole political scene.

The eighth category comprises the vast bulk of the regular executive government. Considerable variety of political exposure may be seen in this category, yet it appears to be of one general kind. The Weather Bureau may be one extreme example of a strictly service agency. In spite of the importance of weather, the Bureau is relatively noncontroversial and popularly supported. Bureau stations are spread widely over the country, and the organization is subject to countless popular interchanges. Its head is politically appointed, and the agency is subject to all normal executive controls. It is subjected to many influences from other governmental organizations, from aviation, agriculture, and similar private groups. Local snow removal and park administration are similarly relatively free of controversy. Many research organizations are normally in a similar situation, yet the Atomic Energy Commission has outstanding political character. The Bureau of Standards is under many commercial and some public pressures. Citizen concern about plant and animal diseases leads to demands on some research agencies. The universities and land grant colleges are political forces with which governmental research agencies must reckon, and industry penetrates most research activities with its interests and pressures.

In the field of social research, political character is more obvious. Crop reporting and price forecasts of the Bureau of Agricultural Economics are under constant fire, labor studies and income distribution studies are hotly argued and have led more than once to cuts in appropriations. Who shall be Commissioner of Labor Statistics is a question fought over by labor unions and business, and the various reports of his bureau are widely argued.

The bulk of the action activities of the government are even more widely exposed. The "fixing" of traffic tickets is a common corruption of government which results from the close association of local government and citizens. Assessment of property comes so close to citizens as usually to be very weakly administered. At the federal level, policies and activities of the Bureau of Reclamation, the Forest Service, the Bureau of Mines, the Soil Conservation Service, the Postal Service, the Bureau of Internal Revenue, the Bureau of Indian Affairs, the National Park Service, the Fish and Wildlife Service, the Bonneville Power Administration, the Rural Electrification Administration, the Civil Aeronautics Administration, the Bureau of Foreign and Domestic Commerce, the Conciliation Service, the

Employment Office, the Civil Service Commission, the Social Security Administration, the National Housing Agency—all these and many others extend widely through the country and come in direct dealing with millions of citizens.

As the government has taken on new activities, the job of carrying them on has been extended throughout the country, the personnel and agencies there to be pushed at, nagged, coöperated with, resisted and resented, cheered on, played off against each other, given opportunity to compete with each other for favor, attention and funds.

The Department of Agriculture is an assemblage of agencies of this kind. A count made some years ago showed 13,000,000 pieces of mail received in one year at the Washington offices alone, and an equal number of telephone calls handled. At somewhere in the neighborhood of 10,000 field offices, the mail and telephone and personal calls were greatly multiplied. Visits at the homes and offices of citizens by employees of the Department numbered millions.

The nature of personal visits, telephone calls and letters is significant. Certainly, the citizens making them felt in most cases that they had policy concerns. The communications represented concerted demands of very large organizations, the Farm Bureau, the Grange, the Farmers Union, the Cooperative Council, large wheat coöperatives, commission men, packers, millers, bakers, the Land Grant Colleges, State Commissioners of Agriculture, and bankers. There were pressures from Governors, party leaders, individual members of Congress, Congressional committees, the Department of the Interior, the State Department, the T.V.A., the Treasury Department, the Budget Bureau, the Department of Commerce, the Department of Labor, and of course requests of the most diverse kinds from millions of farmers. Most of these requests and demands had to do with administration having policy significance. Arguments about the application of policy are essentially arguments about policy. Actual operations are conducted on a field across which mighty forces contend; the forces constitute policy situations. Administration is constantly engaged in a reconciliation of these forces, while leadership exerts itself in that process of reconciliation and through the interstices of the interlacing power lines that cut across the field.

4

The point here is that this is the eighth political process. It is a popular process in which vast numbers of citizens participate, in which assemblages of citizens comprise power units contending with each other, in which various governmental organizations are themselves functional representatives of special interests of many citizens, and in which these organizations themselves contend mightily with each other in the course of working out a consensus that translates many special interests into some workable approximation of public interest. This process is as essential to the evolvement of governmental action as public debate, and closely akin to it.

In this process are visible checks and balances not envisaged by our early architects of government. For our government has not simply grown big, it has grown big in a society grown big and great. Education and franchise have been much extended. Parties have developed. Newspapers have multiplied, radio has appeared. Senators now are popularly chosen. Primary elections are numerous. The Presidential candidates are more popularly chosen. The extension of government out of Washington to undertake new tasks in direct association with the affected citizenry has made a great difference. Increasing interrelations of governmental programs, putting a new emphasis on coördination, have made executive officials take on in dramatic ways a function of representing citizens in their diverse interests, and reconciling those interests. Relations between local, state, and national governments are far more intimate and complex than in earlier times. The checks and balances of court restraint, and basic legislative control remain; the administrators are acting with regard for what the courts have decided and seem likely to decide; they are acting under general policy determinations laid down in law, under threat of legislative change in policy, under constant scrutiny by the legislative body and under much direct legislative influence. But they act also under restraints of those associated together in the handling of complicated business; under restraints of hierarchal control; under restraints exercised by competing agencies representing other functional responsibilities and points of view representative of other citizen interests; under pressure from affected citizens throughout the jurisdiction and all over the country as they and the officials engage in the conduct of governmental business.

The dealing with policy and the dealing with administration at lower administrative levels has a restricted political character; it has the political character of the dealing between an official and a citizen, or a small number of citizens representing a particular citizen interest and a particular government interest. As the same business is handled at successively higher levels it characteristically takes on successive increments in political character, increments in broad social applicability and total-governmental significance. As business begins to approach the levels occupied by political officers, it comes closer to being truly political business, and closer to the area of the partisan-political. While the vast bulk of the political process by which most of the government's business is handled is wholly non-partisan, civil servants working at high levels need to be able to work effectively with officials who have party responsibility and general political responsibility. The adequate bridging of the non-partisan-political that is the general, daily business of the executive branch to party leadership is a progressive phenomenon within the executive hierarchy, taking on acute aspects at very top levels and requiring there much more consideration than is commonly given it. No sharp, hard-and-fast line exists between the top civil service and the political-officer level; none should exist. The needs at that level, and the realities of the relationship between the administrative process and the special partisan function need much study and exposition. This will be the subject of the next lecture.

CHAPTER III

Partisan Politics and Expertise

It is a PRINCIPAL function of public administrators to reconcile and to mesh the functions of politicians and the functions of experts in the service of society.

In spite of the ill repute and common misunderstanding of politics, there is in this country no constant or strong tendency to fail in practice to recognize the importance and value of political control of our political affairs—government. Businessmen may say, "We need a businessman for President," or scientists may say, "We need a scientist," or economists may bemoan a President's lack of economic training, but no interest or functional group would long consider turning over our political leadership to any group other than their own—except to politicians. This is a reassuring and significant fact.

One has only to visit a county court house to be struck by the prevalence of a certain type among

elective officials. They look up eagerly, expecting
to recognize the visitor, ready to give him a hearing,
hoping they may be helpful and at least wishing to
make plain their desire to be helpful. They re-
member names and faces. These attributes are representative in a simple way of those that qualify for
political functioning.

1

Political parties do, above all else, two things:
They provide machinery for developing majorities;
they develop, elevate and identify the "compleat"
politician for various roles of political leadership.
The politician is the preëminent, practicing governmental generalist. Some politicians can function
well as such only at relatively low levels; rare ones
of enormous public value can function well at high
levels. Some are fitted chiefly for legislative posts,
but a few—notably some who rise through governor-
ships—can provide much better political administrative leadership than men in other fields reputed
to be great executives. Indeed, many times when
political leaders are popularly credited with being
"great leaders but poor administrators," the ap-
praisal reveals a failure to understand the nature of
the administrative job at the level in question. The
professional administrator who makes such judgments is akin to the economist who bemoans the
political administrator's lack of equipment in eco-

nomics; he would make chief political administrators in his own less-political image. The top political administrator is not to be judged by professional-administrator standards. Those standards apply only to the professional administrators. The political administrator is preëminently the political and organizational synthesizer.

Few fields have or require really analagous figures. There is none, for example, in the strictly economic field, having to do with the rationalization of everything economic. Only for economic *segments* is there similar leadership. In the general field, final reliance is on the "invisible hand," on supply and demand and competition. For that reason the economic order as a whole has a more mystical character than the political order. The politicians do constitute a kind of priesthood, for only they seem to have the ability to read on the scale of politics the weights of their kind of demand —innumerable and different sentiments—simultaneously and in a fluid context. As a priesthood, however, they are readily unfrocked, and they operate in fields of keen competition. While they serve, they serve all specialized fields, such as the field of economics, so far as those fields are dealt with by government.

Top-level administrators are generalists, too. The best ones in government service closely approach the politicians in ability to weigh forces, sentiments and demands. They somehow especially "understand the country," or large parts of it; such understanding, indeed, is the crucial essential to superior public administration. They, better than anyone else, understand the politicians. They understand experts, too.

The functions of top-level administrators are "more political" than the functions of lower-level administrators because they relate to more of the total-governmental area, to more citizens, to more governmental organizations, to more of the political processes. The higher the attainments of public administrators, consequently, the more "generalist" their performances, the more interchangeable they are with respect to assignments, and the more their functions have to do with weighing popular and organized forces. Such functions are not expert but synthesizing.

Some of the ablest of top public administrators have held "political" appointments not involving public political roles or direct party relationships. Two recent directors of the U. S. Bureau of the Budget have been cases in point. Temperamentally very unlike, one was slow in decision and movement, the other incisive and quick in the same particulars. One was trained in engineering, the other in law. The engineer had spent his life working in and with government, the lawyer a few years as a Congressional secretary and more years in industry. Both were extraordinarily distinguished by social attitudes, and intellectually strangely alike. Neither qualified as an intellectual-type person as that phrase is commonly used; neither could formulate very well what he knew, and neither could have been said to "know as much about the government" as a good many of their subordinates. Neither knew as much economics or political science as many of their subordinates. Neither could deal at length with political or economic theory. Yet both were practicing and practical philosophers. Both knew and understood people and the country. Both had organizational sense. Both had in high degree the rare and priceless intellectual quality referred to by Brooks Adams in the following paragraph, which surely reflects a conception of the intermingling of policy and administration:

Administration is the capacity of coördinating many, and often conflicting, social energies in a single organism, so adroitly that they shall operate as a unity. This pre-supposes the power of recognizing a series of relations between numerous special social interests, with all of which no single man can be intimately acquainted. Probably no very highly specialized class can be strong in this intellectual quality because of the intellectual isolation incident to specialization; and yet administration or generalization is not only the faculty upon which social stability rests, but is, possibly, the highest faculty of the human mind.

2

Just below the level of such political public administrators are to be found strictly civil service administrators of similar and only slightly less political quality. Other men in the Bureau of the Budget dealing with the entire national government
know the government more intimately and are important contributors to synthesis. Generalists in
function, some generalize better in language and
some better in action. Their weighing of the public
political scene is done with a general understanding
of the popular scene but chiefly in terms of the pressures within the government as representative of
pressures working on the government. In various
agencies are administrators of similar abilities applied chiefly to their governmental segments but in
terms of the governmental complex. Some bureau
chiefs and some departmental staff officers comple-
ment each other admirably in departmental service.
The bureau chiefs are oriented principally toward
segments of the public interested in or affected by
the bureau programs, while the staff officers are
oriented principally toward the reconciliation and
integration of the bureaus with each other and
with other organs of government. A departmental
budget officer, for example, is characteristically on
guard with respect to things that will make trouble

with Congress, and on that account is preliminarily concerned about what will make trouble with other departments or with the Bureau of the Budget.

As business moves up the hierarchies—first of a bureau, then of a department, and finally of the executive branch—then, it undergoes progressive translation from special-interest and specialized substantive and expert consideration, to more general, more total-governmental, more total-public, more completely political consideration. The movement upward for particular business may cease at any level, according to the degree of consensus achieved, according to acceptability, according to popular concern. Any particular business may, when popular concern is sufficient, emerge at the level occupied by political officers. Whenever partisans see in it grist for the mill whose job it is to try to create a majority, it emerges at the partisan-political level. The partisan-political element in government is the governing rudder—but only that. It derives from the desire to win elections, which is a desire to secure majority support. This, of course, is basic to popular government and in general roughly motivates search for courses of action in the popular interest.

The executive government has little partisan character. This is the sense in which politics and administration may be most sharply differentiated.

3

The smaller and more local the jurisdiction, the greater tends to be the partisan character of executive government. In a county of small population, the proportion of elected officials is highest, and assistants tend to be more readily appointed on a personal or patronage basis. In one-party jurisdictions, partisanship generally has freer play, and government generally has fewer political values of other kinds.

Even in a one-party, machine-ridden city like Memphis, however, one may believe that both party and machine are less partisan and regimented than is commonly believed. Some of its employees are expert enough and have sufficient standing to reflect credit on the organization by their presence on the job; their presence is all the machine can get from them, and the machine prefers that to the subservient loyalty of less capable or less outstanding persons. Other employees are engaged as a group, their qualifications being union membership rather than machine membership. Others are the rare and valuable persons who keep the wheels of the various departments turning smoothly and who are, for all practical purposes, really indispensable. These employees go their own ways, vote as they please and speak about as freely as the rank and file of Memphis. (Even leading business men usually weigh their words carefully when they speak about Mr. Crump.) Even in Memphis, I repeat, it is most probable that a considerable number of the city's employees act and speak about as freely as citizens at large do. If citizens feel that they can't speak freely enough, the problem is a general civic problem, not simply a problem of bureaucracy.

In a city less tightly controlled, the percentage of employee independence undoubtedly is higher. Where election outcomes are uncertain it becomes highly necessary to administer affairs so that employees have little ammunition to give to the opposition. Strict party or faction control of personnel would be a political boomerang. Here the effort must always be to avoid vulnerability, at least to keep things going pretty well, and to avoid doing things that can seem to be dictatorial. The larger the city, the larger the administrative organization must be; the larger the organization, the greater is the necessity for retaining experienced personnel. The more nicely balanced the political situation, then, and the larger the city, the smaller is the turnover as one party or faction takes over from another. Firemen, policemen and school teachers comprise a large part of the body of municipal employees; they, union laborers, and key, experienced office personnel are little affected in tenure by changes in administrations. Even without civil service, in the largest modern cities most employees are neutralized, rather than mobilized, with respect to partisan politics. Changes in administration affect principally the occupancy of a relatively small number of key jobs.

State administrations generally compare in this respect according to their size and cosmopolitan character. They tend to be rather freer from partisan color than smaller cities and counties.

In the Federal government, there is least partisan character. Even under Jackson, as Arthur M. Schlesinger reports, "the most careful estimate is that between a fifth and a tenth of all federal office-holders were dismissed during Jackson's eight years, many for good reasons." Marquis James says that Jackson left more than 9,000 out of 11,000 untouched. Today, if another party were to come to power it is most improbable that as many as one per cent of Federal personnel would be changed as a consequence of the party change. A considerable number of these are not in key "policy" places—United States marshals, district attorneys, regional or district collectors of customs and collectors of internal revenue, and certain postmasterships. (These postmasters constitute the largest single group, in spite of the fact that a very high percentage of postal service places is under civil service.) Those subject to direct and arbitrary change in Washington are to be numbered in the hundreds, and these are, for the most part, in key positions capable of affecting performance considerably. As vacancies occur in the normal course—as in judgeships—several hundreds of places would be filled with persons having affiliation with the incoming party. Yet altogether the whole number of appointments affected would be an extremely small part of the total personnel.

In the Federal government it is impossible to mobilize more than perhaps ten or twelve thousand for partisan political action. An effort to go beyond that group definitely in the patronage sphere would be known at once and would induce more hostile than favorable political action. Jackson Day Dinners of recent years in Washington, for example, never brought out more than a thousand or so, and by no means all of those were executive office-holders, or even office-holders and their wives. Many were from the legislative branch, from party committee staffs, from business and other interest fields. A number were personal—rather than party or jobholding—friends and followers of the President then in office.

A study of election figures in precincts suburban to Washington, where Federal personnel predominate, will disclose the fact that in those areas the vote distribution follows closely the national vote distribution, with a small deviation rather consistently on the conservative side. In normally Democratic territory, precincts where Federal workers are numerous vote much more Republican than the surrounding Democratic territory, usually producing a result very slightly more Republican than the national Republican vote percentage. It would seem that Federal workers at large vote almost exactly as citizens in the same income brackets vote nationally. It would appear, then, to be a fair conclusion that whatever contribution Federal workers may make to policy, it is not associated substantially with partisanship. The belief is being stressed in these papers that administrative personnel do make important contributions to policy but of a kind different from the partisan. Whatever policy change is in response to party change is effectuated in non-partisan action under the leadership of the relatively few partisan officials.

Effective service of partisan officials is highly dependent on non-partisan officials in key administrative positions. Transference of business from the partisan atmosphere to the civil service atmosphere is full of difficulty of communication. This difficulty normally is minimized by the utilization of a few semi-partisan and a larger number of wholly civil service aides on the basis of a kind of congeniality that is in some part intellectual, in some part perhaps chemical. Time has demonstrated the need of political officers for such hand-picked aides, and the importance of their functions. The more fully "political" civil servants can be at this level, short of partisanship, the more useful they can be. But many elements of personality, related to personality factors in the partisan officials, also are important. The result is that while some civil servants survive many leadership changes, there is on the whole more rapid turnover and change of assignment for top-level civil servants closely associated with partisan officials than for any other professional group in the government. Even under the same leadership, as public conditions change, these civil servants move in and out of the leader's personal orbit, up and down in favor, in and out of the government.

This kind of turnover in recent years probably has attained greater dimensions than ever before. It has been much greater than the change in partisan officials as Department and Agency heads. This turnover is a political phenomenon, and only very moderately a partisan phenomenon. In five successive administrations the Executive branch has been controlled by one party. Changes just referred to, therefore, can be explained only in part as a product of the dynamics of administration *per se;* they would appear also to reflect changes from depression conditions to war, from war to peace and post-war boom, from Roosevelt to Truman, from a situation in which Congress was strongly Democratic to one in which Congress was strongly Republican, then again Democratic. These things involved politics, principally non-partisan; they involved policy shifts; they involved administration. And they had such impact on administration and administrators as to demonstrate the intermingling of policy and administration.

4

In a large way, the role of experts in the process of administration should have become generally clear in the course of this discussion. It is a role auxiliary to the role of administrators, as the role of public administrators is auxiliary to that of politicians. The relationship of experts to the administrative process does require some further attention, however.

At lower levels in the administrative organization occurs the simplest joining of expert and administrative functions. Relatively simple but specialized information there characteristically is brought to bear on action directly involving a small number of people. At each successive level up the hierarchy more varied bodies of specialized information are brought to bear on action involving a larger number of people. The weighing of people—their demands, needs, likes and dislikes—and the weighing of different sets of facts expertly developed are involved at each level, but the process of weighing, that is the arrival at judgments, characteristically has to do with more complex materials and broader application at successively higher echelons. Expert functions become broader, too. The handling of a program in a county involves dealing with county geography, for example, while the handling of the same program at a regional level involves regional geography. Community economics similarly gives way to national economics, commodity economics at a higher level merges with national income economics. Expertness has its own hierarchal structure and application. But at every level, expert service is auxiliary to more general, more political, administrative judgment and control, until administrative judgment becomes auxiliary to political-officer, legislative or partisan or popular determination. Any particular problem is capable of being pushed upward for resolution by political processes. It is less likely to be pushed upward, as a general thing, if it directly affects only a few citizens, although charges of injustice to even a single citizen on some occasions have become national issues. Except where modified by leadership, the height of the level at which attention is given to a problem is roughly a product of the dissatisfaction of citizens, multiplied by their number and strength, modified by their geographical-jurisdictional location and by their persistence and techniques of agitation.

Administration has very much to do with the weighing and reconciliation of popular forces and sentiments. The higher the level, *in general,* the higher appears to be the degree of complexity of

contending forces and sentiments forming the core
and the context of an administrative problem. The
more these things are true in respect to any particular problem, the "more political" and "less expert"
becomes the task. The height of the level at which
expert analyses are determining, relatively determining or directly useful appears generally to be
inverse to its political content as thus described.
Where or insofar as the more-political officer or
body moves in, the expert moves out; where the
more-political official delegates or defers to the less
political, the expert scope expands.

The more aspects a problem may be seen to pos-
sess, the less directly does an expert contribute to its
solution. Insofar as very broad problems, heavy
with content, are actually or theoretically susceptible to multiple analyses of multiple factors, the
more determining function involves the bringing
together of all these analyses and their evaluation
together. The more-political are the aspects of a
problem, the more this function takes on a character diminishingly dependent upon expert analyses.

There would appear to be some justification for
the generalization, therefore, that expert contributions tend to be most directly applicable at lower
administrative levels, where a problem can be
made relatively simple, relatively specific and relatively free from varied, varying and intense sentiments of those involved. The more variables in-

volved—and particularly the more wholly political those variables (the more they involve intensities of diverse sentiments), the more difficult is it for the expert to make more than an incidental contribution. So it is that normally the great body of scientists associated with action agencies experience greater frustration as they try to deal with successively higher hierarchal levels. So it is that high-ranking administrators and politicians often are impatient in the course of their attempts to secure from scientists useful contributions to the solutions of social action problems.

Several qualifications must be entered to these remarks, of course. First, it must be recognized that the level at which expert contributions may be made effectively is influenced by the political prestige attaching to experts and their contribution in reference to particular problems at particular times. With the growth of scientific knowledge and its dependent technology, the public will come to rely more and more on expert contributions—although never to the extent or with the finality experts expect. Second, it should be recognized that expert contributions made at many low levels in the administrative hierarchy flow upward in that hierarchy. Third, generalist experts functioning in or associated with higher levels help to increase the utility of the flow of expert materials from below and make important semi-expert contributions of

their own. Fourth, selected experts may work effectively close to such generalist experts, and par-
ticulary on some types of problems having national
impact and importance but relatively high specific-
ity. Some tax studies are excellent examples of such
contributions. And, finally, contributions of the
scientists will move toward maximization as the
scientists learn better to direct their curiosities to
studies having wider and higher applicability. But
in any case, so long as they remain scientists they
will have less-political functions, and high-ranking
administrators and politicians will continue to exercise the more-political functions. And, with trivial
exceptions, only the politicians will have partisan
functions.

All administration and all policy-making within
the government are political, being governmental,
but only a small part of either, by mass, has identifiable partisan character. Nor does all partisan activity have direct bearing on either policy or administration; much of it is auxiliary activity, related to
the maintenance of parties in readiness for their
special participation in the processes of governance.
Within the executive branch political forces are contending, preliminary to or in prevention of their
being handled by parties. Agriculture, labor and
business in particular are large and distinct political
forces. Many of the issues they present are administratively resolved; many must be administratively

resolved to leave the function of parties a reasonably manageable one. It is not quite true to say that administrators handle all political issues up to the point where they become partisan matters, but they go far in that direction. A more valid statement is simply that—at the national governmental level, for example—administrators handle all policy up to the point where it gets Congressional attention. Even in Congress not all policy questions assume partisan character. The parties are essentially reserve mechanisms for generalizing and simplifying issues, narrowing and clarifying range of citizen choice. Administration deals with more numerous, and on the whole more specific and more detailed issues. Administration deals with more complicated issues in the sense that their detail reveals complications.

The process by which administration deals with these matters is a process of up-and-down movement of materials within hierarchies, and horizontal movement of materials between hierarchies. The structure of these hierarchies and the structure of their relationships have important bearing on the process. These things are next to be discussed.

CHAPTER IV

Structure, Hierarchy, and Co-ordination

Except for the policy question of whether there shall be a government at all, the most basic public policy question concerns the form of government. Every subordinate policy question similarly has, at every level at which it is treated, its corresponding question of form—of character, and of manner of effectuation. The policy decision to have an enlarged defense program is meaningless until the policy is given concrete form in a certain kind of defense program. In the giving of form to such a policy, some of the factors are technical and involve specialized evaluations of relative appropriateness; some are political, involving evaluations of popular persuasiveness on the one hand and of the effects in international relationships on the other; some are administrative, involving specific evaluations of feasibility and manageability and equally involving general evaluations of political, technical and managerial factors together. A small and relatively subordinate unit dealing primarily with location of defense bases must give consideration to all these factors Congress must consider in making its broader determinations.

1

The parts of an organization having to do with program have to do with administration, and the parts having to do with administration have to do with program. In all those parts, policy-making and administration are one operation. The significant fact is that an organization is merely the means for dividing work. If it be granted that an organization is policy-making as well as administrative, then policy-making may be expected to be divided widely in the organization as administration is divided widely in it. We are dealing here with institutional performance, and the principal source of trouble is that there is too little understanding of organizations.

Government is above all else an organization. As an organization dealing with matters of concern common to its citizens, it is at once the nurturing source and the product of the society. Big business could not have developed without big government, and the development of big business requires the development of big government. A complex society and a complex government are necessary complements. The most complex society is a multiple-organizational society. A multiple-organizational society offers most in the way of individual differentiation. In our society the great majority are today highly dependent upon the functioning of many organizations, and peculiarly dependent upon the functioning of the government, yet the study and understanding of organization are embryonic.

A one-man business may involve many functions, many kinds of policy-making and execution. The same kind of business grown to require a thousand employees sees the operations enlarged and both policy-making and execution divided. The operations are not normally simply what they would be if they were a consolidation of a thousand one-man businesses. The thousand can do things acting together they could not do acting separately. The significance of the whole enterprise is in the division of labor, and labor is divided in two ways: operations producing the product are divided, and operations managing the undertaking as a whole are divided. In the organization of a thousand persons there are not only new opportunities, but there are also new problems of relating the parts of the operation, new problems of decision-making. The thousand are not merely assembled, they are given form, organized. And the form in organizations of human beings is universally some form of hierarchy. Among chickens it has been referred to as the "hierarchy of peck."

If the organization we have been considering takes on new functions, it becomes still more complicated, its policy and managerial problems still more numerous and more complicated. It accordingly requires hierarchal changes. If it establishes branches, and if it reaches out geographically for supplies and clientele, its policy and managerial problems become further complicated, and further hierarchal arrangements are necessitated.

Hierarchy is the means by which structure is given to human organizations. Organization and structure are related terms. There is no organization without structure, and structure is an important determinant of the nature of the organization. Such determinants are policy-making. In the government, hierarchy—if we include in that term, as we should, the legislative bodies and the courts—determines and does everything that government does. Work is divided, but all of the parts are interacting. Hierarchy within the executive branch, as a part of the whole hierarchy of government, has its own profound importance.

Structure is a primary concern of constitution-makers. Yet structure and administration are terms as closely related as organization and structure. Organization exists where there is structure, and administration is possible where there is administrative structure; administration takes place through structure, and if there were no administration government would be a discussion club, if, indeed, it could exist at all.

2

Factors determining the nature and performance of an organization may be listed as these: membership, control, purpose, resources, powers, restrictions on powers, conditions under which powers may be changed, structure, physical and social environment. All of these factors determine structure. All of them affect policy. These factors differentiate organizations. We might ponder, for example, the extent to which the vesting of sole power in the United States government to coin money and fix its value and to wage war differentiates it from all other organizations in the country. These factors also are elements of resemblance. They always imply: some kind of formal or informal charter; consent by those associated and maintenance of inducements for followership; some dependence, at least, on sentiment outside the organization; dependence upon history, convention, precedent; dependence upon leadership; use of some kind of hierarchy related to purpose, powers, and restrictions on power.

Organization is a product of, and itself furthers, division of labor. But once created it directs the divided labor, and it is also devoted to preserving and directing consent. Hierarchy provides for movement of work problems and materials upward and downward to achieve consensus or consent within the organization and consent within the community. In the case of government the organization includes all citizens, but there are necessary special consensus formulations within the government organizational personnel concerned as well as within the constituency. In one sense of the two words, the New York State government arrives at consensus—agreement on a course of action—within itself and within New York, and achieves consent within the United States; the United States government achieves consensus within itself and within the United States; and achieves consent in the world community. Actually, in large organizations, intra-organizational consent is more often achieved than consensus. It is used as approximate consensus, or in lieu of consensus. The business of achieving consensus and consent is participated in by administrators and administrative agencies, legislative bodies, courts, parties, agitators, and voters. All of the eight political processes are involved.

Hierarchy is the vehicle of action and decision on which the processes work. It functions both perpendicularly and horizontally. The horizontal relationship is between units and between agencies, commonly regarded as coördination in an effort to distinguish between coördination and administration. Coöperation effected between units responsible to a single executive is coördination at the level of the units, administration at the level of the executive to whom they are responsible, whereas he in turn participates in coördination with other agencies at his level. In the end, all decision-making in the executive branch is administration, and it is all, or nearly all, coördination too. Following the logic of this distinction, the relationship between branches of the government involves coördination rather than administration, the whole governmental hierarchy not being unified at the top. Actually, the relationship of the President is somewhat definitely subordinate to Congress as a body, in terms of actual power possessed. Some offset is involved in the fact that the President's powers are the powers of one person, and the powers of Congress are so divided among 531 members in two houses that it is difficult there to establish equal unity, and consequently difficult to arrive at precise agreements on courses of action and to exercise precise controls. When members of Congress are agreed, their powers are superior. The total governmental hierarchy, therefore, includes legislative bodies and courts. They are all affected by hierarchies in politics, hierarchies of organized parties and interest organizations. They are all affected by the various political processes.

Within the executive branch, general functions of hierarchal structure include the following: fixing responsibility; providing leadership with areas of discretion at successive levels; providing means of exerting influence and exercising followership; making any particular organization and the general executive government manageable; making it acceptable; determining levels at which decisions of various kinds may be made; providing for ready movement of decision-making from one level to another under agitation; bringing to bear relevant, competing and complementary interests, functions and viewpoints. More specifically, it is the means by which resources are apportioned, personnel selected and assigned, operations activated, reviewed and modified.

In the operations of hierarchy, levels are of great importance, although the word has unfortunately invidious connotations, suggesting intrinsic inferiority and superiority whereas the reality has to do only with hierarchal relationships. Levels in organizations are not fixed strata, but are tentative and flexible locations of various kinds of responsibilities and functions. Individuals and units occupying certain scalar levels rise and fall in "importance" according to urgencies. But identification of levels is essential to the operation of hierarchies.

Perhaps the first significance of levels lies in the division of work perpendicularly and the consequent organization of work in terms of the supreme administrative commander and his responsibility. It is no more possible for the supreme administrator to perform all necessary policy-making than it is possible for him to perform all other work of the organization. Even if it were possible in terms of his capacity, as it certainly is not, it would not be possible in terms of organizational psychology. All other members of the organization are human beings, not robots, and in their various responsibilities they would require, and they would inevitably exercise, policy-making discretion.

Actually, of course, it is not possible at any higher level to have all of the information possessed at the next lower level, and it would be the height of absurdity to imagine that all of the information available everywhere in a large organization could be available to, or used by, the administrator at the apex. The abstraction at each successive level of information needed and useful at that level is of the essence of administrative performance.

The only important "duplication," to use a word frequently heard in indictment of government, at all common in any large organization is the duplication that occurs when officials through inadequacy overlap the levels below them. Parallel duplication —the performance by different units of the same functions, is extremely rare and temporary; organizational rivalries and protection of jurisdictional prerogatives keep related programs somewhat too far apart, characteristically, and the need is for more delicate coördination and interweaving. As one young bureaucrat once expressed it, the need is to make a mesh of things.

3

In the upward and downward movement of business, the basic question at each level is this, "What do I need to know that will enable me to exercise the kind of judgment for which I am responsible?" There is even a good deal of virtue in a more negative question, "What can I forgo knowing and doing and still exercise the responsibility appropriate to my situation?" A principal difference between a top-level executive and a low-level executive, if they are well placed, is in the much greater ability of the former to arrive at valid judgments on highly selected information. This faculty goes along with an ability to exercise judgment about many more kinds of situations. Such judgment turns on situational relationships.

In terms of the level next higher, an appropriate, basic question is, "What do I need to report to my chief?" This question involves another, having to do with the form of the report. To pass upward to level A from level B a memorandum which came from level C is normally inappropriate, even though only a small percentage of the C-level memoranda are thus passed on. In most cases the level next higher does not need all of the information, and in many cases the need at the higher level is in part for different information. Yet it is true that each member of an organization needs to report to his superior officer a little more than enough to meet the needs of that officer, so that both the subordinate and the superior may be certain that the superior knows about and has access to everything essential to his judgment.

A very simple but vivid example of this process may be given. It is the story of a New York businessman, the vice president of an industrial company, who was told by the company's president to "run down to Washington and see the President." The errand had to do with a matter in which the President was certain to have a strong, personal interest. In Washington, the visitor called on the telephone, in succession, each of the persons on the White House staff whose names he had ever heard, but he could reach none of them. Knowing the nature of his business, I assured him that he would get an appointment with the President if he simply told his story to the girl on the White House switchboard. He did, and had a most interesting half-hour with the President. The operator said to herself, "I'd better tell the chief operator about this." The chief operator thought, "I'd better tell General Watson's secretary." The secretary thought, "I'd better pass this on to the General." The General said to himself, "It sounds as if the President will want to see him; I'd better check with the Boss."

Policy often is involved in every step of such transactions.

In its more complicated aspects this exercise of judgment about what to report and what to assign to a lower level is the crux of hierarchal performance. This it is which both enforces and circumvents "procedure through proper channels." A good deal of circumvention is essential, else all business would be handled by an impossibly difficult number of "steps," all of which are theoretically implicit in any organizational chart. It is circumvention that makes the transaction of business possible, it is the chart that makes the transaction of business responsible. It is the *right of access*—rather than invariable handling—that supports responsibility, and it is the exercise of individual judgment concerning the need of hierarchal associates having the right of access on which the whole business turns. That judgment is quickened by administrative sanctions, competitive prerogatives, and the political environment. Learning comes from burning fingers. That which is likely to make trouble, trouble with associates, competing groups or affected citizens, is that which is "checked" both laterally and perpendicularly before action is taken.

The circumvention of proper channels is normally only work simplification, and it is valid when that is what it is. Such simplification is systematized to a degree in large organizations. A common practice is for papers to pass through the hands of persons representing two or more officials or units having "right of access" under formal responsibilities, judgment being exercised at these representative points concerning the need of those officials or units to know about the particular business. Another common device is for business to be referred directly several levels downward for original consideration, to come upward step by step for final consideration. Another practice is for out-of-channels transactions of non-trouble-making sort to occur frequently and to be occasionally and briefly reported.

The problem of channels is illustrated in an especially difficult setting in the case of Washington-field office relationships. If the Forest Service, for example, has in Washington a chief of the Service and eight assistant chiefs, each with general responsibilities over certain segments of the program, and a regional office is headed by a regional chief and perhaps four assistant chiefs covering regionally the eight fields of the assistant chiefs in Washington, each of the assistant regional chiefs would report to the regional chief and to two assistant chiefs in Washington, while the regional chief would report theoretically to the chief of the Service in Washington but in practice to the eight assistant chiefs as well. The problem is to simplify the handling of business and at the same time to enforce responsibility. If all business were to be handled by the regional forester, and all regional business with Washington were to be handled by him with the chief of the Service, neither job would be at all manageable. If all the business were handled by assistant regional chiefs with assistant chiefs of the Service in Washington, neither the regional chief nor the chief of the Service in Washington could be responsible. Operations are made both manageable and responsible by exercise of judgment concerning the needs of more responsible officials. In case of doubt, proper channels must win; responsibility comes first, for work simplification that breeds irresponsibility is not at all truly efficient.

The movement of business upward within a hierarchy and laterally between hierarchies is a movement toward a greater and broader consensus. In arriving at this consensus, parts are played by more information, more points of view, more functional prerogatives and responsibilities and exposure to more popular forces. This exposure of business results in substantial program modifications—policy changes. A very high percentage of lateral coördination has its only need in program adjustment to other programs; while this is administration, it is administration with 100 per cent policy content. Actually, treatment upward in a unified hierarchy involves program adjustment in the same way, adjustment to other programs in the field of the higher responsibility.

4

Absence of trouble in any particular business is the usual index of consensus, and the signal for stopping the upward movement. Intensity, location and scope of critical attitudes are the usual measures of the lack of consensus. These measures give signals calling for consideration of business at higher levels. Consensus, the lack of it and the degree of lack, with respect to any one activity becomes a factor in the whole political complex in which majorities are constituted or dispersed.

Work-flow studies normally have to do technically with the ease and simplicity of physical performance of work. Consideration of the flow of work here is given in terms of its relationship to policy and to responsible and popular control. Control is normally thought of too exclusively in terms of prevention of venality, maintenance of generally uniform practices, or, at best, maintenance of power. Although administration is often thought of as an end in itself, it finds significance only in programs, the carrying on of which is the task of administration. Control here is considered, therefore, in terms of programs. Hierarchy is the essential vehicle of such control, and hierarchy is provided by structural arrangements adjusted to environment and function. Control, through hierarchy, means positive things—ability to get adequate reports, to judge performance, to fix responsibility, to make programs responsive to social conditions, and to establish organizational environments most favorable to most desirable decisions.   So-called housekeeping functions and so-called administrative management are subordinated in this view to general administration, which is devoted to the carrying out and development of social programs.   Efficient administration is that which is socially desirable and acceptable.

Management of the flow of work upward and downward within human hierarchies and between human hierarchies is the art of administration. Management of that process in a political environment within a governmental structure providing for various political processes is the art of public administration.   It makes distinctly democratic contributions when the political structure and institutions are democratic.

Part of the democratic contribution is made visible when controversy flares within the government. The government needs most of the time and finally to find agreement, but preliminary to that it needs also to identify issues, and to serve as an arena within which issues are resolved.   The executive branch has its own parts to play in these functions; it furnishes many of the causes and many of the gladiators. The frequency with which controversies within the executive branch get the headlines is a demonstration of the continuing policy-making contributions of the executive branch generally. Differences less dramatic than those making the headlines are bread-and-butter business for administrators. It is business that is a product of political vitality. Public controversy is simply a moving up of the level of treatment of some particular matter. Anything done within the executive branch can be so moved up if there is sufficient concern about it. Members of Congress generally and members of the opposition party in particular, the press and interest groups are trying continually to dig out matters for higher attention; they are continually nominating issues as "candidates" for that attention, and citizens vote by reacting or failing to react to these various nominations. Those matters not "elected" are administratively resolved.

In the posing of issues, and in their resolution, executive agencies perform a certain representative function, additional to the functions of other representatives of citizen interests. The Bureau of Reclamation, for example, is a special representative within the government of areas and interests concerned with reclamation. Its influence with Congress is not its own, but that of citizens concerned about reclamation programs. It is not merely representative, of course; within certain limits it is also the government of the United States in matters having to do with reclamation. In its operations it has to balance the interests of the Salt River Valley and those of the Imperial Valley, the Hood River district and Wenatchee, the different interests of Colorado and Idaho. Within certain limits, its balancing of these interests is a translation of special interest into more general public interest. The limits are at the points where the Bureau ceases to be "the" government of the United States and becomes only a small part of it. At those points the Bureau comes under the collateral influence of the Indian Service, the Division of Power, the Bureau of Land Utilization; at those points it comes in competition with these and other bureaus of the Interior Department for public funds, in competition with the Corps of Engineers, the Department of Agriculture and the rest of the government. At those points it meets the Interior budget-making process, the Interior administrative leadership, the Bureau of the Budget, the President, the Appropriations committees and the whole Congress. In the process, reclamation policy is more and more influenced by other agencies representative of other interests, and in the end reclamation policy broadly, and very specifically in respect to funds made available to effectuate it, is made by Congress.

5

In the whole process, many hierarchies play parts. So do informal organizations within the formal ones. The emphasis here being given to formal organization is not intended to ignore informal organization but to offset somewhat the enthusiasm of those recently arrived at "discovery" of non-hierarchal association and communication of personnel. Reference here has been made repeatedly to human organization, implying full recognition that the members of organizations are human beings with diverse and complex characteristics, their interests and lives ramifying far outside the bounds of any hierarchy and through the interstices of hierarchy. Just as government by law and government by men are not separable, so administration and persons are everywhere involved together, so persons in informal organization and in formal organization together effect and affect the business of the organization.

A very valid approach to administration can be made exclusively in terms of the management of persons organizationally associated, and any such treatment would have to give much consideration to informal organization. But for this discussion the effort is to recover something of the peculiar significance of formal organization as the systematic and responsible vehicle of administration. Formal organization and its hierarchy have added significance as providing character and place for specific informal organizations. Informal organization, in other words, is here more or less taken for granted, non-intuitive learning about it up to now being regarded as having chiefly technical, managerial and internal significance. Its principal significance externally in relationship to policy-making within the administrative process has to do with the fact that it raises impediments to conspiracy on the part of administrative personnel. This is true because many persons have to know about almost anything done within the government, and because government personnel talk with extraordinary freedom.

Impedients to conspiracy, however, are provided by the very fact of hierarchy, particularly hierarchy in a political atmosphere and hierarchy subject to political review and control. The fact that complex work of concern to many people has to be apportioned, its performance participated in by a good many individuals and units having different preoccupations and responsibilities, tends to make venality difficult. Specific legal, legislative, popular and administrative techniques add other difficulties. Informal organization, with all its potentialities for spreading rumor in an arena where opposition party, press and interest groups are ready to capitalize on hints of wrong-doing, does provide an important, additional safeguard. Persons in government jobs, placed in an environment particularly favorable to free talk with associates and with acquaintances, take great advantage of the opportunity in those jurisdictions where strong, one-party partisan control does not impose a special discipline. This kind of discipline is not at all characteristic of the national government, but it does operate in some places on the lower levels of government.

Complex hierarchy exists where the work done is especially complex, and a distinguishing feature of complex hierarchal organizations is the formally coöperative character of their work. Where much coöperation is a necessity, the chance for conspiracy, relative to the whole performance, becomes small. Coöperative work in small organizations can be largely informal, and in such circumstances personal congeniality and group cohesion can become high. In large organization, the very fact that coöperation has basically to be formal tends to make for more representative performance, a performance less likely to be dominated by one individual and managed by him in isolation from his associates. Competitive units make much of remarks overheard, of the identity of callers and friendships, and the grapevine carries upward through hierarchy questions about individual attitudes and qualities of performance. It is one of the functions of hierarchy to appraise such questions.

In any case, the operations of a hierarchy are important in getting decisions made on a basis representative of diverse points of view. A relatively simple picture may be painted by considering a particular program activity as it is conducted within only four hierarchal levels. Beginning at the bottom, let us assume twelve units comprising 120 operating agents, ten in each unit. There are twelve supervisors. Each supervisor and his ten agents might operate in many different ways if they were free agents, removed from any other organizational influence. The performance of the unit would be generally along lines acceptable to and in some degree determined by each member of the group. But the fact that there are twelve such units means that while each individual will influence his unit, each unit will also influence every other unit and all the individuals concerned. This influence is formalized by the fact that each of four executives directs three supervisors of units. Each of the four executives facilitates adjustment of the three units under his direction to each other. In the process, he injects his own influence, which is a product of his own personal qualifications and his exposure to and responsibility for the whole situation of the three units. Each of these four executives, in turn, is influenced by the other three. The result at this four-executive level is an interplay of give-and-take among 120 agents, twelve supervisors, and the four executives, and the consequent emergence of policies and practices more representative of the whole situation covered, and more responsive to the total public exposure of the organization. The four executives in turn are responsible, however, to a single executive, who further influences the whole business in terms of his entire responsibility, his exposure to the public, and the fact that he in turn is responsible to another executive whose responsibilities and outlook are still broader. Complicate this by lateral influences from associated groups and consolidated responsibilities of all these groups to still higher executives and wider publics, and the picture approaches normal, large-organizational reality.

All of the persons associated in this hierarchal arrangement have, among many characteristics, the desire to be liked not only by their associates but also by their friends outside the organization and by citizens with whom they work in carrying on governmental business. The desire to be liked by citizens with whom they deal is heightened by the capacity of those citizens to make trouble for them by writing letters to legislators and high executive officials, and by complaining in the community. The higher one is placed in the hierarchy, the wider the citizen exposure and responsibility are, and the more the desire to be liked and applauded extends to larger publics. A considerable part of the function of a higher level is to insist upon having account taken of all the citizens affected within the range of that higher level. Taking account of all the persons in the hierarchal structure contributes to this function, as well as being itself another function.

An individual in handling government business with a citizen adjusts that business, within his area of discretion, to that citizen. In these adjustments he is limited by having to deal also with other citizens, he is limited by directions from superiors, by his own sense of policy and public responsibility, and by his anticipation of trouble he would invite from the public and his administrative superiors by an excessive deviation. His superiors, regarding a larger public, would lay down rules reflective of more varied citizen situations, insisting by implication upon the interests of others than those known by an individual agent. The agent would refuse in some degree to follow directions in making application to individual cases, and in general would keep his superiors aware of the type of cases he had to deal with. Often he would protest that his situation would not permit compliance with certain directives.

6

Administration is, within rather wide limits, this application of policy generally formulated in law. Successively, the application is made more specific by policy formulations applied to particular publics, made still more specific by application to smaller publics, and finally to individual cases. Conversely, it is the formulation and application of policy in particular cases made more and more general at successively higher levels representative of successively larger publics, until at the highest executive level the President is representative of the whole American public. Administration is in very large measure these two processes carried on simultaneously. It involves constant business that is response to criticism, response to social stress, and a reconciliation of competing or diverse interests and felt needs. These things all involve trouble encountered in the process of administration; they lead to program adjustment which is policy adjustment. The job is the same, whether the occasion is a growing situation in popular psychology, or a physical phenomenon which changes the direction of rehabilitation loans to flood relief. Administrative trouble within the hierarchy itself, made evident in differences of opinion, is in a substantial degree a reflection of these outside troubles demanding exercise of administrative leadership in the effectuation of changes in activities. The more serious the difficulties with the public, the wider and deeper the public concern, the greater the stresses within the hierarchy, and the higher the levels at which decision-making occurs.

Principal variations as between governmental agencies, in the ways in which the picture here sketched applies to them, have already been recognized. These variations reflect differences in political character of the agencies, differences in the extent of their involvement in all of the political processes of government.

The Defense Department and the Department of State do not characteristically and generally act upon and in close association with large domestic publics. They are, therefore, outstanding examples of agencies not so directly, variously and precisely subject to informal political processes. Forces generated by families of military personnel and by suppliers do operate on administration. But the end functions of both these departments are for the mass of citizens relatively remote and subject only to rather general popular judgments. Those general judgments are brought to bear chiefly through the President and the Congress, but this less specific and varied impact on administrative hierarchies has the same general character as the popular impacts on other organizations of government. Nowadays, indeed, the State Department provides a most vivid example of policy-making being done in the process of administration and at the same time being subject to widespread agitation. Popular concern with policies of the State department is now so great that a very much higher proportion of decisions made in that department must be made at higher hierarchal levels than in any other department of the national

government.   This poses an extraordinary administrative problem for the State Department.

The administrative hierarchy is an organ receiv-
ing messages of popular demands, many of them con-
tradictory.   It is an organ responding to such demands, reconciling them, and in the course of response injecting considerations of prudence, perspective, and principle, including regard for other
popular demands and aspirations than those expressed in the chorus of the moment.   All this is a political process, much of it completed within the area of
administration.   Administration has this character.
Its better performance within this character is the
aim of all who study public administration.

CHAPTER V

Administrative Power

THE AMERICAN PEOPLE vest in and express through their government very great power. Their increased use of government has carried with it an increased vesting of power. In these papers it is contended that a substantial part of this increased power is inevitably exercised by policy-making in the course of administration. Is the exercise of this administrative power in harmony with democratic tradition and ideals?

1

Modern concern about the possession and exercise of power by government turns principally, of course, on the question of whether checks and balances and procedures in their modern totality are adequate for the continued protection of pluralistic values. There is a sophisticated concern, too, about the government's possession of sufficient power, or sufficiently consolidated power, to achieve often enough and quickly enough agreements on courses of action where action is urgently needed.

It is not intended here to discuss the second question at any length. It does seem desirable to point out that one of the consequences of the first concern and a result of complex organization's own requirements is to diffuse power within the government, to make government so dependent upon delicate interaction between its parts, as to induce very serious and chronic frustration among its officials. This fact, not popularly recognized, should give some reassurance with respect to the reality of checks and balances. Power concentrated in the government is diffused widely within the government. This is true even under dictators. The difference in end-values between a dictatorship and a democracy resides in the absence, in a dictatorship, of the whole complex of enveloping and controlling political processes characteristic of democracies.

The frustration of officials is akin to the frustration of citizens, who feel that the vote is their only participation in government or influence on government. The two frustrations arise in part from wrong expectations, and in part from under-estimation of the reality. Citizens influence government in many, complex and constant ways; they are much more important than they know. But a single citizen should not be able to *determine* what the government shall do, and some of his frustration actually rises from some vague expectation that he will or should do just that. Similarly, an individual member of Congress loses sight of his contribution to the process of achieving agreement as the particular form of agreement he would have liked disappears in a form a majority will accept. The citizen confuses his power with all citizens' power; the Congressman confuses his power with the undisputed power of Congress; the executive confuses his power with the power of "the government." There is in general an underestimation of the importance of helping to make agreement possible and of *contributing* to agreement. Up to the point where this is its cause, frustration is a premium paid for insurance against exercise of arbitrary power by anybody else. Beyond that point, frustrations would indicate some actual inadequacies in governmental machinery.

2

The first part of this discussion, then, will be directed to the checks and balances that insure against arbitrary action by officials within the executive branch generally. In the concluding part there will be some consideration of Presidential and Congressional power relationships. First, we take up these questions: How powerful is a government official? How powerful is a department or a bureau?

These questions may be considered in terms of in-

ternal power, power within the organization affecting associates, and in terms of external power, power
of officials and agencies exerted on private citizens
and on Congress.

Most popular impressions concerning the exercise of arbitrary power by federal government personnel derive from military experience. The impressions consequently are erroneous, for military
agencies rely much more on arbitrary authority than
civil agencies do. Even in military organizations,
concern for personnel grows with time. In general,
in civil agencies considerate and coöperative relationships are as far advanced as in any non-govern-
mental organizations. Personnel in some respects,
in spite of flagrant exceptions, have more security
and dignity within governmental organizations than
personnel in most organizations. This is attributable chiefly, perhaps, to the political character of
government which encourages cautious avoidance
of trouble in a situation where actions accepted elsewhere as within employers' prerogatives may be
made public issues. There is also some tendency to
act so generally by rule and system as even to de-
prive administrators of desirable discretion.

Some field for arbitrary actions is of course implicit in responsibility. In making assignments,
subjective factors are not only inevitable but desirable; and assignments will always be made in some
degree arbitrarily. Nor can all actions of other

kinds possibly be passed on by all who might claim concern. The limits on internal arbitrary action are set by consent and morale, and consent and morale depend upon many subtleties, including social expectations of the time. The degree of urgency attaching to decision-making also affects consent.

A governmental organization characterized by internal considerateness is likely to be more considerate of citizens with which it deals than is a governmental agency conducted within itself on authoritarian lines.[1] Furthermore, the spirit in which a governmental organization is conducted is largely a response to values and mores of the society. For reasons of this kind, not for lack of technical, managerial competence, bureaucracies of nations are far from interchangeable. Efficiency in one society is not efficiency in another. Blunders of a transplanted bureaucracy would appear quickly as blunders in policy. An indigenous bureaucracy is in many delicate and important ways a reflection of its society.

The distinction is valid throughout government. A typical police department in the old South would have internal policies of discrimination against Ne-

---

[1] This is true as well, of course, of private organizations. One department store in Washington is especially known for its accommodating salespeople. Employees of this store report that it has "the best management in town in its dealings with employees."

groes and would make discriminatory policy decisions in external dealings with Negro citizens. A
n o r t h e r n police department characterized by
"tough" internal policies would be characterized
by tough attitudes toward citizens. In both cases,
policies could be changed by either administrative
or legislative action, and in both cases policy changes
would be limited or advanced by popular attitudes.

Personnel within an organization are likely to derive a feeling that its stratospheric head is vested
with vast personal power from the fact that he does
have the power vitally to affect the fortunes of any
single employee. Yet even such power is real only
if it is rarely used in any dramatic way. Limited in
government by law and public relations considerations, it is much more limited by factors of internal
morale. For government personnel generally, allowing for a certain dependence by each one on the
good will of associates and superior officers, their
greatest insecurity comes from political tides (for
the most part not partisan in nature) and the capacity of such tides to force extreme program changes.
Even the glaring exceptions connected with loyalty
investigations are not unrelated to a political tide.
The relative vulnerability of academicians in public posts, and the relative security of business men
in similar posts, are reflections of political realities.

For the most part, popular concern about the
exercise of power by officials reflects fears on behalf

of private citizens. The usual charge that undue power is wielded is brought against agencies as such or against the government in general. It is most often lodged against the national government. Because of its relative remoteness from the influence of single citizens implicit in its dealing with 145,-000,000, it is theoretically vulnerable to the charge. The usual unwillingness of local police to be tough with respect to minor neighborhood quarrels and nuisances is on the one hand familiar, while analagous situations in the national jurisdictions are not observed by many citizens.

Yet specific charges that the national government exercises similar powers unreasonably are surprisingly rare. The actual record reveals substantial defense. Solitary and friendless squatters have been permitted to live out their lives in peace and with much protection on game refuges and other publicly owned tracts. Many cases of trespass which in the case of private ownership would result in quick resort to law are handled by the national government with moderation and long delay. When in a land trade between two government agencies particularly beneficial to Indians of the area, a few Indians deprived of customary grazing grounds cut government fences and occupied the area they had lost, while other Indians also occupied the land newly transferred to them, there were no arrests and no gun-play. Land purchases by the government in peacetime rarely involve use of the right of eminent domain except by agreement, but are effected by laborious negotiation even though owners often feel justified in trying to take advantage of the government. In contrast, police violence against non-violent strikers in Kansas City some time ago is a not unprecedented case at the municipal level. Handling of the bonus marchers in Washington about two decades ago is the only remembered example of that kind of thing at the national level justifying headlines.

It appears, then, that fear of the exercise of arbitrary powers has other origins. Perhaps it is largely fear. Many of the criticisms certainly relate to actions never taken by the government. Two richly experienced Washington executives have agreed in discussing this point that many more persons go to Washington to complain about the government doing things it has not done and is not going to do than go there to complain about things the government actually has done. With respect to what the government may be about to do, rumors fly fast and freely, and some lush businesses are built in vending them. The newspapers characteristically give relatively much more space to speculative stories attempting to anticipate action than to reports of action really taken.

On the other hand, it must be recognized that the fearful agitation of citizens has a value disproportionate to its validity. It is preventive, giving administrators advance notice about what the popular reaction would be if certain actions were to be taken. It is corrective of administration in process. Modification of activities in the light of popular reactions is bread-and-butter administrative business. Actual arbitrary character of actions, then, depends upon whether they are final or revocable, and whether they have been determined by due administrative process. Due administrative process involves consideration of complaints and unfavorable reaction along with other factors, consideration by a process of reaching consensus at an administrative level ready to assume responsibility and to stand on the record in a political environment and under political control.

Some differences in the way in which power is exercised are undoubtedly attributable to differences between agencies in their political exposures. In the sense that the phrase has been used earlier in this discussion, some agencies of government are "more political" and some are "less political," according to the number of the eight political processes in which they are involved, and according to the extent to which they are involved in these processes. Agencies operating in intimate dealings with many citizens through the country are more exposed politically than an agency operating abroad, or an agency having small functions operating only

in Washington. An agency operating wholly outside of Washington, with no head office in Washington, on the other hand, is less politically controllable
by President and Congress than one with both field
and Washington offices. Action in the first instance
will be less arbitrary in an agency much subject to
the whole of the eighth political process (administration), widely and constantly subject to the seventh (agitation), and to all of the political processes
involving the President and Congress, than action in
an agency more politically isolated. Action will be
less arbitrary in the final instance when it also is an
action revocable through further operation of the
political processes.

In these terms it may be observed that—outside
of the military establishment—the larger organizations in the national government are those spread
over the country and widely exposed to citizens and
all or nearly all clearly subject to control by President and Congress. The Post Office Department is
the largest of these, a purely service agency not ever
seriously regarded as a general threat to liberties.
Even the large Bureau of Internal Revenue with its
unhappy and difficult function of tax collection,
while charged with making things complicated, is
almost wholly free from criticism as applying unfair-
ly the tax laws as written. Most of the bureaus of
the Interior and Agriculture departments are far-
flung in close working association with great num-

bers of citizens, and concerning none of these bureaus is there constant, widespread, similar and specific criticism about arbitrary conduct. There are
specific difficulties over specific transactions, but
these appear to be at least no more suggestive of
indictment for arbitrary exercise of power than
similar reports of difficulties with the New York
Central or the Chicago stock yards. In the face of
special efforts by the party not in power and the
press, and in view of the general inclination of citizens in a democracy to complain loudly, and in view
of widely varying situations of citizens under laws
drawn for general application, a large part of the
basic national government would seem by this record to be pretty well absolved from charges of ex-
cessively arbitrary action.

3

There are agencies, however, about which fears
may be better grounded. The analysis, at least,
would direct attention at this stage to the military
agencies and the State Department. Their activities are not carried on as a whole in association with
direct man-to-man effects on citizens generally. Citizen consequences of their activities are general and
indirect, a product of policy (even though much of
the policy may be made administratively), rather
than made visible in administrative association with
citizens. The eighth process here is less fully politi-

cal, in these cases. While they are subject to agitational influence, political control for them is rather
exclusively vested in the President and Congress. A
letter or a 'phone call to the Department of Defense
from any member of Congress is taken more as an
order than is true in the more politically exposed
and sophisticated departments, although Congress
as a whole can control the latter perhaps more easily
than the former. Materials of political judgment
flowing to Congress are much more ample in the
case of the domestic action agencies.

In general, then, certain distinctions with respect
to power and control may be made according to degrees of agency involvement in the various political
processes. An agency may be much exposed to certain political phenomena, and still not be readily
subject to responsible political control or truly popular control. The political phenomena may be too
exclusively of one kind, a product of only one or
part of one of the political processes, representative
of small, special publics rather than of the whole
public.

Regulatory agencies in general may be so described. Because they are regarded as performing
"quasi-judicial" functions, by law and custom they
are more than regular executive agencies somewhat
removed from the control of the head of the executive branch and heads of agencies. They are somewhat especially subject to court review, and of

course they are much exposed to small, special publics. They come in for greatest criticism on the ground of arbitrary exercise of power and general impairment of freedom. But it is difficult to find complaints really directed toward administrative spirit and manner, even in the case of these agencies; the criticisms seem, rather, to be objections to the policies laid down in law.

In this connection it should be remembered that the exercise of definitely police-like powers by regulatory agencies is a very minor aspect of government. It involves a relatively small part of the personnel and funds used by government. Many activities of government are coöperative undertakings of citizens, in which government serves as a crystallizing or operating agent. A city water supply system or a regional power system, or a system of reclamation developments is more a coöperative economic venture of citizens that it is a governmental venture requiring enforcement powers. There is a vast number of other activities of government actually carried on under specific agreements with citizens and citizen groups. And there are many millions of contractual arrangements with citizens, constituting altogether a very great part of the government's business. Some of these are normal, business arrangements between citizens and the government, and some are arrangements involving various kinds and degrees of incentives offered by the government to induce but not to compel certain kinds of action. Others, such as unemployment insurance, while mandatory, involve incentives of such sort as to differentiate them sharply from police-power regulatory activities as ordinarily conceived.

Some of the more outstanding discussions of the Tennessee Valley Authority's program, consequently, have been at fault in seeming to assume that the Authority discovered, originated, or even uniquely advanced administration by means of coöperation and contractual arrangements. There were at the time the Authority was established old-line bureaus with more coöperative agreements and contractual arrangements than the Authority could develop in a limited area. The distinct significance of the T. V. A. has been its application of these techniques in the effectuation of an area integration of program.

The general point here is that working relationships between federal, state and local governments, between government agencies and educational institutions, between government and private research organizations, between government and business firms, between government and citizen groups and individuals are in very great numbers negotiated and coöperative. As Professor MacMahon has said, "The problem of compulsion is lessened by the fact that the control methods of a moving consensus, although pinned initially by majority action at crucial points, will be largely a calculated interplay of inducements, incentives and indirect influences, not direct coercion."[2]

There remain, however, two categories of agencies deserving special mention. One is represented by investigatory, national police-type organizations. Any such organization has capacities for a kind of blackmailing relationship with Congress and executive officials. Whether disposed to use such resources or not, the agency may be given a relatively free hand out of fear. Given especially large appropriations and especially effective public relations, such an organization could be a serious threat to popular government.

Exercise of police power is, indeed, an even more general problem. It seems inevitable that the level of the power of enforcement usually must be the same as the level of power of determination. This was a conception basic to the formulation of the Constitution; in the convention where it was drafted, the crucial determination was to give the new government power to enforce its own laws directly upon the citizens, and not through State governments. This today is seen as the fundamental power which would distinguish world government from an international organization.

In considering the police power, therefore, one emphasizes not need for weakness or for its delega-

[2] *American Political Science Review,* January, 1948.

tion from one level of government to another, but other effective safeguards. An obvious qualification would be in the general avoidance of the exercise at a higher level of police powers with respect to determinations made at lower governmental levels. More subtle qualifications on police powers also are called for in the light of authoritarian uses of the police. This writer is inclined to believe, for example, that large and highly centralized investigational organizations should be avoided at all levels of government, but particularly at the national level; in other words, that the function of police-type investigation should be highly decentralized within the appropriate level of government.

The second special category comprises the very large domestic action program agencies, of which the pre-war Agricultural Adjustment Administration has provided the best example. Dealing directly with more than 6,000,000 farmers, dispensing direct benefit payments averaging over $100 to each of them, determining (as it did in the early 'thirties) the rates of loans on principal farm products and thus determining total income for millions of producers, with some 40,000 people employed and 121,-000 leading farmers (elected by farmers and working rather more for the farmers than for government) serving as community and county committeemen, such an agency could go a long way toward really determining certain public policies. Special administrative provisions making such a special pleader subordinate to the general public interest were required. Any such organization will raise special questions about true and full popular-controllability. But thus far in our history only the one agency in this category has seemed to justify special concern, and the war greatly modified this situation for the better.

Political influence exerted by a normal bureau is political routine, representative of one citizen interest not politically strong enough to pose any special control problem. A few years ago the Bureau of Customs was charged with discharging more inspectors than it needed to discharge in an attempt to force Congress to increase its appropriations. If this were true it would have had little significance, since any drive that Bureau could get under way would be a trivial item in the whole political-pressure scene. Any member of Congress who felt forced to change his vote under such influence would be either a novice or an extraordinary weakling. Charges of impropriety in such a case usually are simply a venting of spleen, a justification of a vote, or a counter-attack—all normal in a situation where forces are contending. An executive branch unable to make its program needs clearly known, unable to pass on to Congress its learning in the course of its political functioning, unable to divert to Congress some of the heat generated in the executive area, would constitute a deprivation of government. Charges of this sort have not seemed to be sustained under any long view, and do not seem to be seriously regarded by mature Congressmen. At the same time, these and other attacks on "bureaucrats" produce great timidity on the part of officials, causing them to deny the duty to be strong in the public interest. Timidity, not boldness, comes to characterize the seasoned public servant.

There is another area, however, in which concern about the exercise of arbitrary power is fully warranted. It has been pointed out that citizen interests weigh in political scales usually in some proportion to numbers of citizens concerned. Any large and widely-spread group is able to gain a substantial hearing. The search for majority support—especially in political situations where majorities are hard to win—tends to carry regard for minorities which are politically effective. But arbitrary action with respect to single citizens, or very small groups, is politically feasible and will be found in practice somewhat in keeping with prevailing habits. Militant action by those not directly affected on behalf of the politically under-privileged is the only safeguard.

It is true, too, that citizen groups and interests of very substantial dimensions may be politically ineffective. The ways in which basic interests are organized within the society may not be favorable to them. The consumer interest, for example, is almost universal, but there is little facility for its organized expression. It is ordinarily subordinated, almost to the point of elimination from the political scene, to the producer or income interest, which is strongly and variously organized. Situations of this kind are the principal source of the most important citizen frustrations. Such frustrations are felt rather vaguely, but they probably account for much more citizen unhappiness than does fear of arbitrary action by the government. Their alleviation can be achieved by citizen agitational efforts or by governmental leadership. Leadership can, in effect, confer organization upon such interests.

4

At the other extreme is the second main area to be covered by this discussion. There the question is this: How powerful is the President, particularly with respect to the Congress?

This is an exceedingly difficult subject, concerning which many prejudices exist. It is difficult because one remark may be couched in terms of a society grown great and complex, and a rejoinder may be made in terms of a simple society. The Constitution-makers could not have foreseen the society of today, and to try to treat the question by imagining what they would think about it if they should return for a visit is futile. Yet it does appear to this observer that the government today is amazingly consistent with the original design, that the design was extraordinarily serviceable in giving shelter and support to a society enabled to develop as richly as this one has developed.

The powers vested now in the Presidential office have changed greatly in scope, as have the powers of Congress. The growth of the society and the growth of activities and responsibilities in the branches of government have gone along together. With a great increase in number of affairs handled, and with increased complexity of those affairs, both the Congress and the President have had to resort to delegation. In recent years Presidents have made many formal delegations to agencies for the handling of matters earlier attended to personally by the President. Similarly, Congress has delegated more decision-making functions to various agencies of the executive government. A remark of Chester Barnard, long-time president of the New Jersey Bell Telephone Company, applies as fully to the Congress (and to citizens) as to the President: "Not to make decisions that others should make is to preserve morale, to develop competence, to fix responsibility, and to *preserve authority.*"

So long as a delegation is revocable, so long as the things done under delegation are subject to review and further direction, power is not relinquished; rather, responsibility is made manageable. No delegation of any other kind has been cited to support the contention that Congressional power has waned.

In much the same way and for the same reasons, powers attributed to the President have come increasingly to be institutional powers—powers of an organization, rather than personal powers. The Presidential office is discussed too much in personal terms, too little in organizational terms. Of the President it is as true relative to his level as it is of any other executive lower in the executive hierarchy that a large part of his role is to effect consensus or to confirm a consensus. He may and often does influence a consensus, but rarely does he determine, and when he does determine he does it within the limits of the organizational and political processes which operate at his level in terms commensurate with his level, as they operate at lower executive levels in terms commensurate with those levels.

In other words, he acts in a situation in which labor is divided, responsibilities are divided and influenced by the whole political complex. His is the chief responsibility, true; just so there are many others with chief responsibilities at many other levels in various branches of the executive establishment. He must defer to the prerogatives and attitudes of those who share responsibility. He acts subject to their coming to a public and violent break with him, inciting diminution in citizen following. He acts subject to subordinates dealing directly with

Congress and playing off Congressional forces against Presidential power. He is the apex of an executive branch so far from integrated that a thoughtful Republican who served as Vice President has said that "the Cabinet members are the President's natural enemies."

A civil servant richer in governmental years and wisdom than any other I know has said in conversation that any man in the presidential office comes gradually to attempt less in the way of tight control, simply because he finds that tight control cannot be achieved. In other words, that President serves most effectively who exercises much less than his theoretical powers, who uses his power as an *ultimate* executive power. It is at that point—and not through the broad exercise of arbitrary, personal powers in a thousand and one directions—that the role of the President is crucial. The Presidency is the top executive level to which the most difficult problems come on appeal from the public in outcries of distress and criticism, the level to which any kind of problem can come when it has grown great enough in citizen concern. It is the level at which major anticipations of national need take form, major responses to felt need are approved. It is the level at which is lodged chief executive responsibility for enlisting popular followership and maintaining majority government. It is a job of such preëminent importance that our political system fails to produce many men well qualified to hold it. But it is the preëminent political job in this country, not a job even remotely resembling that of a dictator. For it is a job in the very center of eight vital and pervasive political processes. They provide checks and balances as undreamed-of by the Constitution makers as the dimensions of our present society.

It is with understanding of the President's role within the executive branch that his power with respect to Congress must be considered. And the relationship must be thought of in realistic, organizational terms. It must be recognized that the very purpose of an organization is to find agreements on courses of action, and that any organization which in the end finds really substantial disagreement of wide scope is on the verge of very serious trouble requiring more drastic remedies than are provided usually in orderly procedure. It is not strange that, in spite of the many years when one or two houses of Congress have been dominated by a party opposing the President, throughout our history Presidents and Congresses have been generally in agreement. Every President has signed many more Congressional enactments than he has vetoed; every Congress has given very serious consideration to the chief recommendations of the President of the time, and a very high percentage of those recommendations has taken form in law. It has been a process of give-and-take, with leadership and compromise on both sides, and the business of finding agreement has gone forward. Talk of a "rubber-stamp Congress" is for the most part silly and uninformed. This nation was 65 years old before Congress passed any bill over a Presidential veto, and 75 years old before this occurred in a substantial case. It happens much more frequently now, not less frequently.

The most novel developments in governmental form in our later history have been of a sort that would make possible a charge that Congress has encroached upon the Executive, rather than the other way around. Beginning in the tragic Johnson administration when Congress passed laws removing the War Department from Presidential control, there have been developments on the Congressional side that would have been undreamed of up to the time of Buchanan. The whole "independent agency" conception has developed in the wake of that Johnson debacle. The General Accounting Office as an arm of Congress has come to exercise a pervasive executive control as readily to be faced with a charge of unconstitutionality as the extreme instance of exercise of executive power. The Government Printing Office not only services the executive branch but exercises executive functions to some degree. A few years ago in connection with the putting into effect of the Government Procedures Act, the Printing Office determined what rules and procedures were to be given official publication.

Similarly, the Congressional Committee on Printing exercises a thoroughly executive type control over executive printing. Commissions established by law to determine what particular tracts of land should be purchased for wild life refuges and additions to national forests have comprised both members of Congress and representatives of the executive branch. In many informal ways, committees, sub-committees, committee chairmen and other individual members have attempted quite precise controls of executive actions. Yet none of these is "the Congress."

Actually, however, the general exercise of powers, in terms of the present scene, and the general relationship between Presidential power and Congressional power, seems to be substantially according to basic Constitutional conceptions.

It would be difficult to see how any responsible citizen could fail to recognize the need to have Congress able, when sufficiently agreed, to stop the executive branch, including the President, from doing any particular thing it strongly desires not be done. It seems to this observer clear that Congress does have that power today as truly as it ever had it, and that Congress is enriched for the performance of its functions by the development of all of the eight political processes by which the rest of the government also has been enriched.

Although a reasonable case might be made for leaving the Congressional role primarily that of exercising a veto power, similar in effect to the role of the British Parliament, few in this country actually would argue against Congress also having the positive role of finally determining the policy that takes form in law. This means in positive terms having the power to enforce upon the executive branch particular policies upon which Congress is substantially agreed as requiring such enforcement. Congress surely has this power, too, as from its beginning. It exercises the power as a regular thing, often determining matters of detail having incidence at very low levels in the administrative hierarchy. Some reforms would be desirable, such as the elimination of irrelevant riders, so that Congressional consensus might be more truly required on separate enactments, but the fundamental power of Congress is under attack in no important area of the executive government. The function of Congress is essential to the political complex by which we have found our way until now.

5

Administrative power, widely diffused and much more widely influenced and controlled, is just one aspect of governmental power. The power of the government is coöperatively exercised. To a considerable degree it is self-controlled by the interaction of its own parts. But this is so because both the parts and the whole are politically controlled. The problem of power here is less that it may be arbitrary than that it may be unwise. Numbers of participants do not insure wisdom. A free people is free to go wrong. If it remains free, however, it is free to correct its mistakes.

Administrators share with all others in places of responsibility an obligation to keep the way open for modification and correction. Revocability of decisions bearing on fundamental values therefore becomes an important criterion. The wise administrator will make decisions that are flexible and revocable. In spite of the fact that there is momentum in decisions, and a kind of cumulative logic, the record shows high revocability. Not many questions are capable of being addressed less freely than is necessary in order to determine upon changes in direction which, if held to, could bring our society completely about-face. The danger that we may about-face is perhaps as great as any other. The people could force it, or the people could consent to it. It could not be forced upon an unwilling public. The great and determining power of this nation is with its people.

Administrators share with all others in places of special responsibility the special obligations of leadership. They can, in all innocence, contribute to organizational practices and forms elements which are inimical to popular government. They can help "take things out of politics"—or take themselves too far out of politics. They, like citizens and legislators, are capable of yielding too much to the prestige of military or other experts, too little to the politician who is the central factor in civilian control and popular government. By dealing with the legislature too directly, they may undermine and confuse executive responsibility; by the same tactics they may inadvertently substitute control by members of Congress for control by Congress as a body. By failing to be imaginative about legislative needs, attitudes and prerogatives, they may overburden, and thus degrade, the legislature. Their special duty is in part to help clear the way so that the other parts of government and the other political processes may function well.

If "the end pre-exists in the means," public administrators, by carrying on one of the important governmental means, share with legislators, jurists, party workers, pressure and citizen groups and citizens generally responsibility for nurturing the values achieved and yet sought through American government. Any of those who share it may well be happy that it is not theirs alone. Those who have special, official responsibility have special need for deep insight into the American political community and its institutions.

CHAPTER VI

Liberal and Conservative Administrative Shifts

IF POLICY AND ADMINISTRATION are inter-mingled, it would appear that identifiable differences exist between administration in a liberal regime and administration in a conservative regime. Civil servants rich enough in years to have gone through several sharp policy shifts are well aware of administrative differences between the two situations.

Liberalism has meant different things at different times, and in any period its meaning is far from precise. The discussion here relates to the most common understanding of the word in the last fifty years.

1

Perhaps the clearest modern distinction between liberalism and conservatism is found in this fact: a liberal administration is generally more inclined—and a conservative administration more disinclined—to do new things and to change old ways of doing

things.   In this century the new things liberalism
generally has favored have been things in restraint
of privilege and things thought to be directly beneficial to the underprivileged.   Administrative differences in the two cases are implicit in policy differences.

Administrators in a modern liberal regime will
be more attentive to pressures from popular groups
than they are in a conservative regime.   Persons
and units within the government inclined in that
direction will rise in favor and influence; their potential will find fuller chance for expression. More
important roles will be open to the poor-devils' ad-
vocates.   Civil servants not consciously liberal will
respond to new evidence of public need and expectations.   In the shift, farmers will be relatively more
favored than bankers, workers relatively more favored than employers, consumers relatively more favored than producers, small business relatively more
courted than big business, small taxpayers relatively
more highly regarded than large taxpayers.   In the
eyes of the opposition all this is "rabble-rousing,"
"confidence-shaking," "appealing to the mob,"
"sheer politics," or "vote-buying."

Similarly, liberal regimes are likely to engage in
practices which may be described as "extending the
administrative franchise."   The policy implications
of administrative devices for drawing attention to
groups   theretofore   politically   underprivileged

should be obvious. Setting up local advisory committees in connection with a program of aid to tenants in the purchase of farms was one such practice in recent years. It enlisted the attention and support of key farmers having liberal attitudes, gave them vested interests in a program not directly beneficial to them, and furthered acceptance for the whole undertaking. In the Rural Rehabilitation program, loans to establish small coöperatives of very low-income farmers gave those farmers an opportunity to become vocal as a group. The effect was heightened by making loans sufficient to pay poll taxes where such payments were prerequisite to voting. This was policy-making, and it was management of a loan program.

A specific example of an "extension of the administrative franchise" (with policy consequences) may be cited out of the Department of Agriculture experience:

Section 310 of the Packers and Stockyards Act authorizes the Secretary of Agriculture, "after full hearing," to prescribe changes in the rates charged by stockyards and market agencies that perform services in connection with the sale or purchase of livestock at the yards. Over a considerable period of time following the enactment of the Packers and Stockyards Act in 1921, a practice grew up whereby informal negotiations were customarily conducted between stockyards owners or market agencies, on the one hand, and representatives of the Department of Agriculture, on the other hand, with respect to rates. These negotiations usually related to requests by the stockyards owners or the market agencies that they be permitted to increase their rates. If it was believed in the Department that a proposed rate increase was justified, the Secretary of Agriculture would issue a rate order. In the absence of an agreement, the matter would be made the subject of a formal hearing before a representative of the Secretary, at which the bureau administering the act and the stockyards owner or market agency would be represented by counsel and would present evidence bearing on the reasonableness of the current and the proposed rates.

A question was raised as to whether this procedure was proper inasmuch as it did not afford the livestock owners who paid the rates any opportunity to be heard.

Although the governing statutory provision provided that the exercise of the rate-making authority by the Secretary of Agriculture should be conditioned upon a "full hearing," the statute was silent as to the persons who might insist on the right to be heard at such hearing. Hence, it was a matter of statutory construction to determine whether livestock owners did or did not have a legal right to demand an opportunity to participate in the rate proceedings. It was concluded in the legal opinion which was rendered on the point that the rate payers and those who render the services are equally interested in the rates and charges assessed for the services; and that the interest of rate payers in the determination of a reasonable rate is such that they, along with those who collect the charges, should be afforded an opportunity to be heard in any rate proceeding under the Packers and Stockyards Act. This opinion was the subject of considerable criticism from stockyards interests, and also to some extent from administrative personnel of the Department, because it interfered with administrative discretion to dispose of rate cases without formal hearings. The opinion resulted in farmers and stockmen getting a better "break" than they were apt to get under the previous system.

Related administrative developments in the liberal regime of the 1930's included the establishment of more citizen consultative relationships, exposing to new groups aspects of the formulation and execution of programs. New combinations of citizen interests were administratively developed, too, bringing more widespread support to programs serving new needs. In the Farm Security Administration, for example, where it was recognized that lack of adequate medical care kept many farm families in relief status, a health program was developed which made for physicians paying customers of persons who otherwise would have been charity cases. County and state medical associations joined in effectuating and supporting this program, which was a policy development within the general rural rehabilitation policy.

Similarly, the school lunch program and the "stamp plan" were administrative developments of a more general program for disposal of farm surpluses. The stamp plan combined the self-interest of food dealers, welfare agencies, farmers and citizens in need of relief. The school lunch program had appeal to farmers, many school patrons, nutritionists and the needy. Administrative ingenuity devised the programs and made them successful. That ingenuity was a product of a generally liberal regime. Both programs later were enthusiastically endorsed and specifically authorized by Congress.

One more example may be cited to illustrate the fact that different policy positions are possible in administration—and legislatively accepted—under a law which is itself not changed. The case has to do with a policy opinion of Fowler Harper, now of the Yale Law School, when he was Solicitor of the Department of the Interior, interpreting the portion of section 9 of the Reclamation Project Act of 1939 (43 U. S. C. 485th) relating to the minimum rates to be charged by the Secretary of the Interior in the sale of electric power generated at reclamation projects. This opinion has been the subject of a great deal of discussion in Congress and elsewhere during the past few years. A successor to Mr. Harper, Mastin G. White, reconsidered the opinion after he became Solicitor of the Department, and he concluded that it represented a reasonable interpretation of an ambiguous statute. A description of the matter follows:

Subsection (a) of section 9 of the Reclamation Project Act of 1939 indicates that, before a reclamation project is to be undertaken, it must be determined that the receipts from the sale of water for irrigation and municipal purposes and from the sale of electric power will, together with such allocations of costs as may be made to flood control and navigation on a nonreimbursable basis, equal the estimated cost of constructing the project. Subsection (c) of that section provides that the Secretary of the Interior, in the sale of electric power, shall fix rates which "in his judgment will produce power revenues at least sufficient to cover an appropriate share of the annual operation and maintenance cost, interest on an appropriate share of the construction investment at not less than 3 per centum per annum, and such other fixed charges as the Secretary deems proper." A question rose as to whether the law required the Secretary to fix rates for the sale of power, which would, as a minimum, return to the United States during the period of the useful life of a project an amount equal to the share of the operation and maintenance cost properly chargeable to power, the part of the construction cost of the project to be repaid from power revenues, and, *in addition*, interest at 3 per cent per annum on the part of the construction cost properly allocable to power. The proponents of a vigorous public power policy in the West contended that such a construction of the law would result in rates at levels sufficiently high to interfere with the widespread utilization of power generated at reclamation projects.

The Solicitor of the Department of the Interior held that the law did not require that the rates be fixed at the level indicated above. It was his opinion that the minimum requirements of section 9 relative to rates for the sale of electric power generated at reclamation projects would be complied with if the Secretary of the Interior, in connection with a particular project, should fix rates which would produce annually power revenues at least sufficient to cover the share of the annual operation and maintenance cost of the project properly chargeable to power plus an amount equaling not less than 3 per cent of the part of the construction cost of the project which has been allocated to power, subject, however, to the further requirement that the annual power revenues over and above the operation and maintenance item must be increased beyond the 3 per cent figure if it is necessary to do so in order to produce during the period of the useful life of the project an aggregate amount equal to the part of the construction cost of the project that is to be repaid from power revenues. This interpretation has been hailed with approval by those who favor cheap public power, and it has been violently criticized by others, in Congress and elsewhere. Either view is supportable.

This happens to be an example of policy-making based on a formal interpretation of law, but countless other examples could be provided where administrative flexibility would not require any conscious or new interpretation of law. In the particular example, policy was not "made" by the Solicitor of the Department, but he helped in the making of policy. In another administration the opinion rendered by Mr. Harper could have been presented, but the policy might not have been accepted. The point here is that discoverers of certain opportunities to establish or to shift policies in a certain direction are more sought, recognized and elevated in one administration than in another. Yet when any position is taken, it will be a position concerning which personnel in the operating bureau, in the other bureaus most interested, in the Solicitor's office and in the Secretary's office have achieved acceptable consensus. Congress in both cases also would be informal party to the consensus—at least not agreeing on a disagreement.   Policy shifts of the sort here described can be, and are, made administratively, and in either the liberal or the conservative direction.

A liberal administration, then, gives more room to imagination, boldness and ingenuity than does a conservative administration.   It tends to give principal attention to movement toward objectives newly seen.   The conservative administration tends to give principal attention to the support of objectives long familiar.   These differences affect the administrative process generally.   But they do not make either the liberal or the conservative type administration either more or less venal or more or less efficient than the other.

In an extremely narrow sense of efficiency, one concession might be made to the conservatives. In an engineering sense, no new organization quickly attains high efficiency.   Since liberal administrations give birth to more new organizations or undertakings than do conservative administrations, there is a sense in which conservative administration is more efficient than liberal administration. But how can we weigh in terms of true social efficiency that kind of performance against the effectuation of new political adjustment to new conditions which is more readily achieved under liberal auspices?

Variations in kind of administration have the same ultimate justification as variations in kind of policy.   Kinds of policy and kinds of administra-

tion alike and together are shaped on the anvils of
politics.

2

Effectuation of the shift from conservative to liberal position, or from liberal to conservative position, poses a great administrative responsibility for
policy. It is a process less exposed to view but quite
as important as the shifts in Congress and White
House. If the social shift is substantial, the bureaucracy tends at first not to move so far or so fast as
country, President or Congress. If political forces
continue to operate in that way, the bureaucracy
gradually picks up speed in the new direction until
at some points it is politically checked. In a second
shift in governmental position, the bureaucracy
again retards the movement. It is in the long run
a check on liberalism, a check on conservatism, but
a servant of both because it is politically located,
conditioned, and controlled.

As older programs refine themselves they serve
in some degree the development of social efficiency.
New programs as responses to new felt needs are also
servants of social efficiency. Relative efficiency of
the two, consequently, is a question of criteria. To
a person of liberal convictions, liberal administration is more efficient than conservative administration; for a conservative the opposite is true. Chester
Barnard's remark that there is no objective test of

efficiency except survival here has special applicability. *Political* efficiency is the final criterion of every aspect of government, and the ability of our government to shift position in accord with changes in social needs and sentiments has much more to do with our social efficiency than any engineering measurements of any administrative processes.

In a perfect political order (including a completely adaptable administration) the *political* efficiency of liberal and conservative types of administration would be identical, the one being as perfect a response to felt need as the other. Since opinions about relative efficiencies of the two turn on opinions about what is desirable, and since the two performances have the same kind of difference as the two contrasting political attitudes, they are essentially political phenomena. Which is "better" or which is "worse" then becomes a question involving not administration alone, but *all* of the political processes by which the government lives and acts. In a large way, which is better and which is worse is dependent upon and determined by the popular consensus of a particular time. Government at any time should be a reflection of that consensus as determined by agitation and leadership.

Public and administrative confusion connected with the shift from a conservative regime to a liberal one or from a liberal regime to a conservative one would appear to be roughly a product of the rate and extent of the changes in either direction. Confusion in Washington and confusion about the government in the country in 1945-46 would appear to be very much greater than the confusion in 1933-34 when the policy shift was in the other direction. But the shift in the latter part of the first Truman administration, involving a 49 per cent reduction in personnel and other changes not reflected in that figure, was absolutely much greater, too.

Not all the refining of "administration" is a product of conservatism. Personnel administration in departments and agencies was much advanced in the early nineteen-thirties, and public administration as such got more extensive and intensive attention in that period than ever before. In some degree this was a product of simple necessity implicit in the growth of administrative organizations and problems. In some degree it was a product of an increase in the area of discretion open to leadership. That area of discretion is greater in times of emergency and stress than in stable times.

On the other hand, the original establishment of the Civil Service came about almost without regard for the liberalism or conservatism of the administration of that time. It was a product of public education and agitation given point by the assassination of President Garfield by a job-hunter. As an administrative development, in other words, it was a quite typical product of politics—a response to a need become strongly felt.

Changes in policy, effected in the course of administration, are a sequel to elections, anticipations of elections, reflections of changes in leadership, and reflections of changes in popular feeling. Substantial changes take place within the duration of a single Presidential or single party administration.

The Farm Security Administration, for example, operated under one unchanged law, under one President, but under four different administrators; it changed substantially in each case and very greatly under its fourth administrator. All of the policy changes were administrative. Some involved substantial change in clientele, attention swinging from very low-income to moderately low-income farmers. All of the changes were made below the level of Presidential direction, and below the level of Congressional determination. In part they reflected an accompanying shift from more liberal to more conservative administrative leadership. In part they reflected and anticipated changes in Congressional sentiment later crystallized in a new law.

3

In a general way, the liberal or conservative character of administration is a direct product of the political consensus of the time as modified by leadership. A graphic view of the matter may be approached if we depict popular political attitudes as a kind of spectrum with red representing extreme political radicalism of the time at the left and violet representing extreme reactionism at the right, and if we depict "normal" distribution of political attitudes across that spectrum in a normal curve. This may be done pictorially rather than statistically in somewhat this fashion:

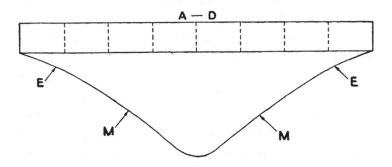

In this diagram, the line AD represents the area of discretion available to political leadership in "normal" times, the area around some point in which a majority consensus of consent may be effected. More or less of that area may be utilized, according to the imagination, ingenuity, strength and persuasiveness of the leaders of the period. Leader-

ship may be exercised more at the left side of the
area, or more at the right, according to the attitudes of leaders, their interpretations of the form of
the sentiment curve then existing, impending or
susceptible of effectuation. In such a situation as
here depicted, popular agitation at points M, represented by the Moderates, will have maximum direct
effect, and agitation at points E, represented by Extremists, will be largely disregarded and without
recognizable, immediate effect. The area AD is ap-
proximately in line with the center of the sentiment
curve where a majority consensus is or may be constituted and its location is susceptible to influence
by agitation capable of shifting the point of consensus. The diagram may be regarded as depicting
the political situation in 1928 and 1929.

Under especially stressful social conditions, the
distribution of sentiments undergoes change. Bom-
barded by events, magnetized or repelled by leadership forces, driven by internal desires, influenced by
agitation and social psychology, the human particles
possessing sentiment attributes are relatively scatter-
ed into a new distribution across the spectrum, and
perhaps more often than not shifted perceptibly
leftward. If there is inadequacy of leadership, or
particularly if there is an inadequate shift of leadership in the area AD, a new adjustment in the area of
discretion will come lagging through political campaigns and elections. By 1933, for example, the at-

titude distribution could have been diagrammed
in this way:

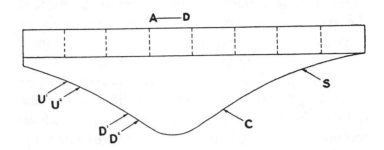

In this diagram the area of discretion for leaders
is left of its location in the earlier diagram, reflecting a shift in the popular sentiment curve relative
to the same political spectrum. AD is wider, reflecting the flattening of the popular sentiment curve
and the correspondingly wider area from which a
majority is to be constituted. (This width made
room, for example, for accommodating both Jesse
Jones and Rexford Tugwell.)

Agitation, in the situation depicted, also undergoes change in effectiveness. The more extreme
sentiment areas on the left, now bulking larger, are
more important to a possible consent consensus, and
agitation at points U^1 and U^2, representing the
areas of the Utopians, the Unemployed and Underprivileged, is now much more effective. At points
D^1 and D^2, representing the Dispossessed and Dis-
tressed, very great influence is exerted, offset con-

siderably by fears of the Cautious effective at point
C. Sentiments of the Secure at point S have at this
time little more political effectiveness than those of
the Extremists in the earlier diagram. Agitational
efforts frequently are not shifted in terms of possibilities for effectiveness just as leadership often fails
to make adequate shifts.

The general picture is completed if we add a diagram reflecting a sentiment shift to the right. It
can be regarded as a depiction of the sentiment
situation in 1946. With war weariness prevalent,
with employment and national income at record-
breaking levels, there is a heavy decrease in consciously liberal attitudes, and a corresponding increase in conservative attitudes. The educational
effect of recent liberal experience probably leaves
for the earlier part of the period at least a propor-
tionately larger spread of liberal attitudes. The
consequences of that liberal experience may be
heightened after a nostalgic return to more conservative attitudes, but for the time being there is
a substantial and crucial diminution in liberal
strength. Concern about international policy or any
similar factor not breaking along liberal-conserva-
tive lines makes for a greater diffusion of sentiment
positions, but in a spectrum-and-sentiment diagram
related to liberal and conservative contrasts the effect probably would be only a mild flattening of the
curve. Conservative attitudes normally involve

fewer policy positions altogether, however, and this would make the curve a little deeper. The net of these factors would appear to produce as the third diagram one directly contrasting with the second:

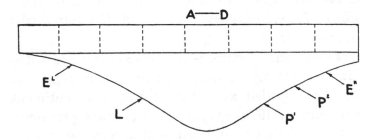

In this situation, agitation at points P^1, representing the Prosperous and P^2, representing the Privileged, would be most effective, and agitation of Liberals would be more directly effective at point L than at points to its left. Attitudes of Extremists at point E^R would be much more effective than in either of the two periods previously depicted.

4

A liberal regime has been differentiated from a conservative administration earlier in this discussion by its greater willingness to do new things and to change old ways of doing things. Both create stresses within the executive branch.

As a whole, however, a liberal shift involves new opportunities for personnel, and the organizational stress, therefore, is not in proportion to the policy shift. When the shift is to conservatism, it is effectuated largely by reductions in personnel and functions and at least a retarding of expansive tendencies in agencies. The shift to the right, therefore, may have a disproportional effect on morale of government workers until such time as relative stability is established, when morale may be at its highest except for the factors satisfying to dynamic and imaginative qualities.

Actually, of course, the location of the political spectrum itself shifts both left and right with shifts in sentiment. The sentiment curve is always a normal curve except in depth—representing dispersals or concentrations of potential majorities. Principal lags in terms of the times are in leadership shifts along the area AD and in shifts of agitational efforts to different points within the sentiment curve in accordance with changes in effective potential.

Particularly appropriate to the present discussion is consideration of the effect of sentiment shifts on the location and length of the line AD. That line is the vantage point of leaders in parties, in legislative bodies, in courts, in chief executive posts. It is a line representing also all of the area of discretion in the administrative process. Popular sentiment shifts involve shifts by administrators and administrative organizations. These shifts are effected, as has been suggested earlier, without much change in personnel dictated by partisan considerations and without very much direct and outright change in personnel altogether. A few hundred persons usually may make all the difference, accompanied by changes in assignments of some thousands of other existing personnel. In a changed climate, with changed leadership, policy develops within administrative organizations generally in keeping with those changes. Changes are not everywhere required, and not made in all areas where changes would be appropriate. Where changes are made, they are not all of the same degree. These things call for more consideration than can be given them here. But the changes made generally result in a rough, approximate response to the changed pattern of popular sentiments.

Within the administrative organization, sentiment distribution at any time is probably very similar to sentiment distribution in the national society. Persons working for the government are themselves members of society, involved in its affairs, influenced by conditions. Any employee is more responsive to new policy proposals in times of social stress, less responsive when conditions are relatively stable. His reaction to conditions and his reaction to popular demands are related. His shifts are accelerated by administrative sanctions implicit in his dependence on leaders. Leaders, in turn, are dependent upon consent of organizational personnel. In various levels and jurisdictions of government the relationships between popular shifts of sentiment and intra-organizational shifts vary a good deal, according to the greater or less political character of the organization, including the percentage of key appointments that can be made outside of the civil service. At the national level, organizational personnel (in proportion to their numbers less directly involved in shifts of party control) appear generally to be more determining of rate and extent of policy shift than at other levels. At the national level, consequently, marked shifts in policy calling for new action are more characteristically achieved through wholly new organizations than through existing organizations.

5

The three diagrams are general pictures of the political situation at particular times. Within some such picture, all of the political processes operate. Public administration, as one of the processes, is auxiliary to the general picture.

Details of any one of the political processes usually would have to the general picture a relationship very hard to trace. Therein lie explanations for much citizen frustration and many of the errors of political students and commentators when they explain very complicated results by over-simplified causes. The general picture is made up of innumerable details. Usually, a good many changes in detail would not alter the general picture, yet the general picture is a product of all of the details. Changes in a few specifics, too important to be regarded as details, a substantial variation in a larger number of factors having general incidence, or slight changes in a great number of small details—any of these conditions usually will result in a change of the total picture. But even the few, important specific factors gain their importance against the background of the whole.

Within the process of public administration, therefore, many decisions involving policy contribute to the general political situation without consequences readily identifiable in that situation. Some of them "cancel each other out," pleasing as much as they offend. All of them are guarded and shaped so as to minimize their special political impact. Many of them resolve political difficulties, and thus prevent developments affecting the general political situation.

Yet any one of these decisions not only is affected by it but in turn affects the general scene. Any decision may emerge as an item somehow requiring higher level modification or reversal; or it may break out as full-blown material for public debate, and may become an identifiable factor in the general political picture. Heads of units or agencies doing much as they have been doing may suddenly find themselves transferred or removed because they had not been imaginative or flexible enough.   Many decisions by individuals, units or agencies slowly make a general picture to which there is an identifiable public reaction judged by political officers to be worthy of action on their part.   Many decisions may throw the balance of an entire administration so that it appears to be more pro-labor, more anti-labor, more pro-business, more anti-business, more this, or more that which is capable of affecting majorities and consent.   All administrative decisions together make up a part of the political complex. The balance between liberalism and conservatism, on the one hand, and the times, on the other, is an important aspect of that complex.

CHAPTER VII

The Influence of the Citizen

IN THIS SERIES of papers, the government has been considered primarily in terms of administration. The effort has been constantly to relate administration to the governmental whole, but of necessity the picture is far from complete. Here we have seen administration as one of the policy-making processes, one of the political processes. The central concern in any general consideration of government must be the citizen, and if the picture here presented is in any way novel we must ask what changes it makes in our picture of the place of the citizen.

This can be done here, of course, only in broad and sweeping terms. The general view taken is that the citizen not only is affected by administration but that he uses it as one of a number of vehicles of policy influence. It is contended that, whatever the citizen's frustrations may be, whatever political improvements may be needed, in this society the citizen is vastly more important than he knows.

1

When an election is over, the average citizen may feel that he has done about all he can do about the government until the next election. Actually, he will vote hundreds of thousands, even tens of thousands of times, before the next election. He will have many more opportunities to vote, but in most cases he will vote by not voting—which is perhaps equally significant. Every expression of opinion on public affairs—in the barber shop or beauty parlor, in a taxicab, at a club meeting, at a party, union meeting, farm organization meeting or wherever— is a contribution to the climate of opinion within which the government acts in its constant effort to achieve or maintain consent. Every withholding of expression similarly is a vote.

Between-elections influence is real, of course, only because there *are* elections. Elections are more important, therefore, than the specific determinations they make.

Between-elections influence is enhanced, too, because of other political processes and institutions that characterize a popular or democratic governmental scene. Free speech and free enterprise with respect to agitation and organization for agitation, are of basic importance. Courts provide barriers to extreme and hasty action, and actually manage many citizen relationships. Many other citizen relationships they influence. Legislative bodies give to the whole government more popular character than they themselves embody or directly enforce. What they might do is as influential as what they do do. A normal two-party situation also makes the individual more directly influential than he would be in a multiple-party situation where negotiators of coalitions take over important processes. A bureaucracy spread widely over the country, there to be pushed at, complained about, incited to action, is another vehicle of popular influence. A competitive bureaucracy, its parts representative of special functional and geographical interests, is another feature; the very complexity of the bureaucracy exposes it to more aspects of American life and interests.

Elections are periodic features of politics. Politics goes on constantly, and so long as democracy survives. In politics—the totality of our political processes—rests the reality of popular government.

It appears that a very great deal of the sense of frustration from which too many citizens suffer springs from an unconscious expectation of too direct and conclusive influence. The individual citizen finds it hard to understand why the government doesn't do what *he* wishes it to do. Or a single pressure group, feeling deeply about some problem, can't quite become reconciled to the fact that the government doesn't accept its particular proposal. Sometimes, indeed, efforts are made to *compel* the government to accept some group proposal. Yet any of us, in a relaxed mood, would agree that each citizen's fair share of influence would be only one-one hundred and forty-five millionth of all citizen influence, and that the government probably should never let any one citizen or any group of citizens write the particular ticket for the exercise of governmental power.

It is the peculiar business of politics working through government to devise responses to popular demands which will gain the consent of citizens generally. Those responses, in the very nature of the process, can hardly ever be fully satisfactory to anybody if they are fairly acceptable to almost everybody. But they can be roughly responsive to the complex of most of the diverse citizen influences. In the long run as they are successively modified in the light of experience and complaint they are so responsive.

In other words, all of the political processes, and not elections alone, are the means by which in this society 145,000,000 people are continually agreeing on courses of action.

In a general way, this is profoundly true. But of course it is also true that power is not uniformly distributed or uniformly exercised. There are differences between individuals, between groups of citizens, and between citizens and officials. There are differences between one period and another, one area and another, one government agency and another.

In other words, it is true that each citizen does not have exactly one one-hundred and forty-five millionth part of all the political influence. Persons too young to vote have less influence than those able to vote. Poor persons in poll-tax states have less than those more privileged. In one-party states or communities considerable numbers of citizens are relatively disfranchised. Persons in especially influential positions of many kinds have more than a per capita influence. This influence is usually associated with some kind of hierarchal status in some one or more of the numerous organizations through which the economy and the society generally live. This points to the well-known fact that organized influence is more effective than unorganized influence.

2

Organizational influences are formulations preliminary to the strictly political formulations. It is a fact too little recognized and considered that the multiplicity and character of private organizations affect profoundly the vitality and representativeness of political processes. The values often sought in proportional representation are better developed in this auxiliary way, leaving to strictly political organizations and processes—notably to parties—the function of converting these complex multiple interest drives into majority formulations.

It is significant that there are in the United States more organizations altogether in proportion to population than in any other nation—and more kinds of organizations. All of these organizations are in varying ways vehicles of political influence. Up to the limits of the citizen's "span of attention" his influence on affairs is heightened and diversified in proportion to the number of his affiliations and exposures and the intensity and persistence of his activity. One index of the differences in political vitality among the states is in the differences in the degrees to which their citizens are organized in multiple ways expressive of diverse interests.

The levels of government characteristic of this nation are themselves one form of this multiplicity of organizations through which diverse popular sentiments are brought to bear on affairs. The number of jurisdictions may be too great, ballots may be too long for the citizen's span of attention, but the general structure of national, state and county and city government exposes government widely to citizen influence.

Strictly political organizations are popular vehicles of especially general and pervasive importance, of course. Taking account of all citizen interests as otherwise expressed, they have the function of generalizing issues, synthesizing response, narrowing the range of choice, establishing majority consensus and/or consent. While a majority position may be established usually and finally only by narrowing choice to two alternatives (and these alternatives usually not markedly different if orderly evolution rather than revolution is to be the course of affairs) successive choices may radically affect social direction.

The influence of citizens is not uniform in any organization, whether it be strictly political or only indirectly or incidentally political. Influence varies according to personality factors and hierarchal status or responsibility. A citizen without formal hierarchal status in an organization may exert a determining influence on an organization on occasion. Another may exert influence disproportionate to his formal status in the hierarchy. But usually persons are more especially influential according to hierarchal position; the president of an organization usually has more influence than its vice president has. Persons so situated are there representative of members generally, and exercise some of the influence of the members. The representative function therefore is effected through series of relationships in and among all of the varied organizations within the society expressive in various ways and degrees of manifold member attitudes. These attitudes are simplified and generalized in the process, and in the process many attitude forces are sifted out. Even so, the remainder is a great variety of competing and complementary organized sentiment drives which derive from grassroots citizen interests and which make up a large part of the material with which strictly political organizations—notably parties and the agencies of government—deal in their turn.

Private organizations are almost always (this writer believes invariably and inevitably) less democratic, less uniformly affected by all whom they affect, than are political-governmental organizations of a democratic society. The socialists Sidney and Beatrice Webb, for example, found long ago that it is unwise even for members of a coöperative organization who are employed by the organization to be permitted to vote on matters relating to the management of their organization. In this sense it is necessary that government be more political than any or all other organizations. It is a special and preeminent function of public political government to deal with and to effect integration of all of these organized interest forces, and more.

3

Politics offers its own representative system, then, in addition to the more or less representative systems of private organizations. Through it, citizens exert still another vital, penetrating and ultimately more determining kind of influence. In this system popular influence on representatives is more constant. It, too, has organizational character, but is has great individual character, too. Because of wide franchise and direct ballot access to those in key positions of responsibility, citizens through elections may spontaneously take positions corrective of those taken by popular pressure groups or by professional political groups.

Because this can and does happen in elections when they go counter to most of the organized pressure noise, it happens also between elections. Politicians and officials are sensitive both to organized pressures present and potential, and to *popular tides,* present and potential. Citizens, then, through diverse private organizations, through strictly political organizations, in the interstices of these organizational influences, and as individuals, are capable of making, destroying or swelling majorities, of causing telephones to ring and lines of action to change in city hall, in court house, in state capitol, in legislative halls, in administrative offices—even in judges' chambers.

In this process special functions are performed by interest groups, opposition party, and press. Democratic government is subject to scrutiny to which no other human activity is subject in anything like equal degree. Interest groups, opposition party and press are the chief investigators. They are continually nominating issues or possible issues as candidates for public attention. Citizens who read or listen unmoved or without definite reaction, as perhaps they must and should in most instances, vote "no." They are consenting to, or not convinced of error in, that which is attacked. If any considerable number responds—and sometimes a very small number is sufficient — governmental adjustments follow. Yet issues of great popular potential—such as public housing in the last few years—sometimes lie fallow for lack of adequate sponsors. Citizens may themselves organize agitational nominations of issue candidates, but too often they leave this role to leaders, to commercial interest groups, the press and opposition party.

4

Everything having to do with the government and everything the government does is political, for politics is the art and science of government. But in terms of mass, only a small part of politics is partisan. In a sense all issues nominated for public attention are also nominated for party attention. But parties accept only those issues which seem capable of being formulated in ways useful to them in affecting the establishment of a majority consensus. Issues of slightly smaller potential or otherwise manageable are resolved in legislatures along other than distinctly partisan lines. A great many issues of still smaller dimensions are resolved administratively. The administrative level at which they are resolved depends upon the degree of specialized character a particular issue has, the size, location, character and attitude of the public affected. A small public deeply aroused weighs more in political scales than a larger public only mildly dissatisfied. Repetition of complaint and demand is an index of intensity of citizen feeling and a nomination for higher attention. Thus about any matter normally handled at a low level in the administrative hierarchy, a militant citizen group can secure Presidential, Congressional or public-debate consideration. This is the peculiar genius of politics. It is in politics—the interacting of citizen sentiments and political institutions as a whole—that exist the limitations on power of officials, and the power of the people ultimately to require any kind of action, positive or negative, about which they are sufficiently agreed.

Two phrases in the preceding sentence have special significance: "any *kind* of action," and "sufficiently agreed." A numerous people will usually be much more capable of agreeing on a kind of action than on the specific form any action might take. The more agreed they are, the more there is consensus, the easier it is to impose on the government the popular will—actually to control the government. The less agreed they are, the more the popular role is to give or to withhold consent. Political processes develop or reveal lack of consensus or consent in the total social context of the moment.

In every case the principal roles of the especially responsible citizens who are officials are: to bring into focus—to resolve and integrate—these popularly-felt needs; to give specific form to responses of the government designed to meet the needs; to inject foresight and concern for factors not readily visible to citizens at large; to try so to organize governmental responses as to secure at least majority consensus or consent. They may make mechanical or automatic responses to popular forces on the one hand, and they may exercise discretion and leadership on the other. The mechanical type of response is itself modified, of course, by the necessity of consciously interpreting public sentiment.

The process produces a kind of political logic different from any other logic, the validity of which is tested or attested by popular consent and governmental survival. As a matter of theory, the process could never be perfect and it can be "rational" only to a degree. It is limited also by the forms of existing political institutions. But it is constantly adjusted by repetitive phases of the process as described, and the process is in a large way reflective of the mixed emotional-reasonable and pluralistic character of a great democratic society of highly differentiated human beings. Even though the process is ever capable of improvement it is confidently felt that no other *kind* of system would so truly reflect and conserve the values long espoused in this society.

There would be grave danger, for example, in straining too hard for "rationality" and minimizing the political, for it is the political that makes room for the whole of human potential, including the rational potential. The world is greatly indebted in this particular to the Labor party of Great Britain for its conscious choice of the parliamentary (political) variety of socialism. In democracy, all social classes, all economic interests, all expertise, planning and power are subordinated to politics.

5

In the United States, popular protection against arbitrary exercise of governmental power resides not so much in any single institution or structural device as in the whole of our political processes, the whole environment of government action. The very complexity of government, the often unclear interminglings of responsibility, the fact that various agencies or organs of government compete, intervene and engage in conflict, is assurance of the existence of checks and balances more pervasive than those formally devised by the Constitution makers. What is done in all other parts of the government is done with regard for what the courts have done and may do; what is done by the courts is done with halting recognition, at least, of what Congress is feeling it necessary to do and what the Executive is feeling it necessary to do. Congress is influenced by the Executive, the Executive act is in conformity with law and constantly restrained and modified by Congress. The whole national government is influenced by state and local governments and *vice versa*. Powers "centralized" in Washington are in reality greatly diffused, among many agencies and divisions of agencies, among many groups of officials, in many places throughout the country.

Within the Executive branch its part of the total governmental power is widely diffused among departments and agencies and among units, among "levels," within units, and among individuals within organizational units—all interacting on each other. Individuals, units and agencies are in certain ways representative of various citizen interests, and as they contend with and influence each other they are reconciling and integrating diverse popular attitudes and interests. Practically nothing done by government officials is done by an individual as a free agent; it is done as a consensus of those organizationally concerned, in an environment of expressed or potential coöperation or interference by other individuals, other units, other agencies, higher levels of control. The interplay of influences within the government goes on in turn within an environment of popular scrutiny, concern, interest interplay and present or potential formal political intervention.

The general result is not a sense of power on the part of officials, but a widespread sense of frustration. They are quite like citizens who feel that their votes are their only participation in government in feeling that their presence in an intricate process is about their only participation. It is hard for them to identify the consequences of their influence on the action product. There can be too much of such frustration, as well as too little. The general situation is probably one of a maximum of such frustration consistent with governmental ability to act; it is generally excessive in amount, rather than insufficient.

Members of Congress as well as executive officials suffer from this frustration. Their constituents tend to feel that their representatives in Congress should be able individually to "control" the government, and they make demands accordingly. Congress as a body can and does exercise a basic control, but its power is divided between two houses, and there divided in one house among 96 members and in another among 435 members. When one house comes to agreement, that agreement is not wholly satisfactory to any member. To secure agreement between the two houses there usually must be more concessions. Congress thus epitomizes within itself the popular process of reaching agreement. Further, Congress as a body, and all Congressmen as individuals, act under strong restraints provided by the political environment, and by other parts of the government. When members of Congress lash out in bitter criticism of policy or executive agency their actions often reflect a quite natural frustration arising from inability to impose their own individual judgments.

The power of the President is greater than that of any other individual in the national government, partly because governmental necessity has so shaped his office, partly because for occasional, major matters the fact that one person's judgment at the apex of the Executive branch is easier to arrive at than the judgment of 531 persons split into two houses. (At the gubernatorial level, the Governor of New York is even more powerful, but in most states top executive power is much less consolidated). This special role of the President is really individual only in extraordinary instances, however, and is then always subject to control of Congress if Congress finds sufficient agreement, and is always subject to popular consent.

In the vast majority of cases, Presidential power is much limited. The President is under the necessity of carrying his own executive organization with him; he must defer to many different heads of organizations with many personal variations and competing functional interests, as they in turn must defer to and be influenced by their associates, by other parts of the government, by their particular publics and by the large public. The Presidential function is in very large part one of securing consensus within the Executive branch in the whole political environment and under checks of all the political institutions and processes.

The general point is simply that Presidential power is greatly restricted and exercised only within a complicated field of other powers and popular controls. Congress undoubtedly still has available every power it had at the beginning if it chooses to exercise it and if it is sufficiently agreed. It can stop the Executive from doing any particular thing it is doing; it can compel the Executive to do almost anything it is sufficiently agreed upon. Any power delegated to the Executive can be reasserted. Indeed, this is done constantly. But the delegation of powers is constantly renewed and expanded, too, since delegation in a more and more complicated world is more and more essential to the preservation of Congressional power. For Congress to attempt to determine too many things in too much detail would be to bog it down and to make it incapable of exercising effectively its basic controls.

Citizens, like congressmen, are often confused and frustrated by regarding the number and complexity of public problems, feeling that they should have a clearer judgment and more constant and direct influence on all decisions. Yet a short ballot does more to fix responsibility and to uphold popular control than a long ballot. And to decide everything by referendum would be to rely on phony and ineffective democracy, causing both citizenship and governance to bog down. The things to search for are arrangements that fix responsibility and provide for popular control when there is popular agreement. In the absence of consensus, democratic government operates by consent, mightily influenced by the possibility of consensus.

Citizens, thus, like Congress, are constantly delegating their powers in order to preserve them. Some they delegate to courts, some to legislative bodies, some to executive officials and agencies, saying each time in effect, "We cannot normally give enough attention to these matters, and we are delegating a tentative responsibility to you; whenever we do not approve your handling of them we will assert our control." The assertion of control is real and is often made. Its commonest form is a flurry of criticism. Sometimes it is the eviction of an entire administration and its party. The importance of criticism is not sufficiently appreciated. Often it is not so such an identification of some stupidity or error as it is a positive contribution to the refinement of government.

It must be emphasized, however, that the sequel

to delegation is the fixing of responsibility and the maintenance of means by which the responsible may be held to account. To these, the too-common popular tendency to approve "taking things out of politics" is hostile; it means taking things out of popular control. This is a frequent device of special-interest groups to effect the transfer of governmental power away from the large public to the special-interest small publics. This, too, is the essence of many pleas for "decentralization." Actually, decentralization is an element in most policy questions—not a separate policy question; it is the question whether any level of government or what level of government should perform some particular function. Whatever the decision is, adequate centralization of responsibility for performance of the function agreed upon at the level agreed upon is essential to popular control. A great deal of administrative decentralization will occur in any case, out of sheer necessity. The Congress has built a significant record of outlawing decentralized, regional offices set up by national administrators concerned only about getting their work done. The record has been built because Congress felt less able to exercise easy control over regional offices. In the same way, Congress hurried to return to Washington agencies like the Securities and Exchange Commission which were pushed out during the war to make room for war agencies. That particular Commission had been located in Philadelphia, and even the Pennsylvania Senators joined in bringing pressure for its return to Washington. Yet Congress in a good many other cases has yielded to pressure groups and legislated administrative forms not lending themselves readily to political control. It is in such cases that citizens should be on guard.

The judicial process is by intent least directly involved in the others and least readily subject to direct popular control. Yet the history of judicial decisions reflects steady, if relatively slow, response to popular "felt need," to use a phrase of Justice Holmes. Where not elected, judges are politically appointed and consequently, over a period of time, politically responsive. They are affected also by actions of legislatures and chief executives as the latter by their actions change the material with which judges deal and the environment within which they act. They are affected to a degree by agitation.

Legislatures and chief executives are most fully involved in all the political processes, and their involvements have been increased through the years. The development of parties, extension of the franchise, the spread of education, the multiplication of organizational pressure groups, the development with Jackson of a special popular procedure for the nomination of Presidential candidates, the change in the role of the electoral college, the popular election of Senators, and the spread of executive government into the country in diverse and close exposure to citizens—all these have been as significant as the growth in size the government has had.

Within legislative branches, members of lower houses, coming from smaller and more specialized constituencies, are more representative of those constituencies and less representative of the whole political scene than members of upper houses. The chief executive is more responsive and responsible to the whole political scene than members of the upper house are. Thus political structure is designed to give representation to local and specialized interests and to provide for their reconciliation and integration into national interest.

6

All of the political processes are *together* important to popular government. It would be absurd to try to argue that the legislative process is more important than the executive or judicial, or *vice versa,* or even that formal processes of government are more important than the informal processes of agitation. They give meaning and content to each other. But the vivid process of party maintenance is perhaps least appreciated and understood by citizens. Just now, with the spectacle of minorities carrying European nations into communism, there is keener appreciation of the two-party system than ever before. We see two parties as the crucial machinery by which majority government is maintained. But great numbers of citizens see the significance of parties only at election time, and seem to expect parties to be maintained in something like a functional vacuum. Parties are notably weak and growing weaker in this country, and in consequence we see more and more instances of bloc government exercised by pressure groups.

Pressure groups are not inherently evil. As a phenomenon they are implicit in democracy. They may be evil, if the ends they seek are evil, but normally any evil products are the result of incomplete functioning of political machinery. The principal inadequacies inhere in party weakness—too little party discipline, too little functional reliance on parties, too few functions for parties, too limited citizen participation in parties. The practical disappearance of patronage at the national level, where normally less than one per cent of the jobs are filled with any chance for partisan considerations to figure, and the steady diminution in relative importance of patronage in state and local governments have left consistent party workers with little prestige, and that little almost their sole incentive. City machines have become the principal and almost exclusive vital organs of party life. They, too, are becoming weaker with diminished functions and prerogatives, and of course they alone are not sufficiently representative of the large bodies of citizens who are nominal party members. How to improve and strengthen parties in America is a major problem.

It should be observed in passing that the word "machine" is generally used as an invective when applied to party organizations. In other words, it is a term applied to a party organization one doesn't like. Yet party organizations are highly desirable and probably essential to democratic government. "Machine" leaders and staff are at least working regularly as citizens—not as officials—at the business of government, which is more than can be said for most of those who sneer at them. Many thousands of them contribute heavily in time and money for nothing but the satisfaction of their public spirit and a sense of personal importance. It should be noted, too, that party organizations tend toward policy neutrality in the first instance; they are instruments of policy-making on which their active members call the tune in an appeal for followers. The party has an open door to those who will play the organizational game. But far too few citizens understand the basic significance and importance of organization as a vehicle of citizenship. It is the negative, non-participating attitude of so many citizens that makes party organizations what they are today. Not necessity but choice makes the ballot appear to so many citizens to be their only means of participating in the business of governance. Such citizens may be said to vote only for the vote and the right to complain. It is their privilege to vote otherwise, and to vote more constantly and variously.

There are also, of course, some important roles to be played outside of party organizations. While very large numbers of citizens should be active and for the most part loyal party members, if all citizens were straight-ticket-voting partisans, registration of voters could serve in lieu of elections, and politics would be far less effective as a reflection of popular attitudes and needs. To have fairly regular partisans maintain strong parties is one thing, but the exercise of total citizen choice between parties and candidates is still another. Existence of a large number of independents and the practice of ticket-scratching make the constitution of a popular majority an ever new phenomenon progressively reflective of change in a dynamic society. With respect to this phenomenon, organizations on the fringe of parties and between parties make special contributions. Somewhat similarly, a third party sometimes may make a special contribution, although at other times its chief direct consequence is to put into power an administration out of line with popular majority sentiments. The threat or possibility of a third party movement often, therefore, is more salutary than its actual entry into the field.

Movements of all kinds that cause the major parties to bid for mobile-voter support contribute importantly to the vitality of politics.

Citizens vote, then, by adding their names and energies to membership rolls. They vote by swelling, or failing to swell, the circulations of particular newspapers or periodicals. They vote by contributing to the popularity of particular radio or newspaper commentators. They vote by writing "letters to the editor." The vote much more potently than they know when they write or talk to members of legislative bodies and to administrative officials. They vote as they express themselves in labor unions, farm organizations, business and professional bodies. They vote in every contribution they make to the climate of opinion in a thoroughly political society. They vote more effectively still as they organize to exert influence. They vote effectively in proportion to the persistence of their efforts, for persistence is an index to intensity of feeling.

Organizing consent and consensus with respect to a very great number of specific problems and with respect to general social direction is intricate business when there are involved 145,000,000 far-flung persons in a society cherishing pluralistic values. A less intricate system would enforce a diminution in diversification of values and would result in a government less reflective of diverse values. A society rich in political processes achieves the logic of a social calculus beyond the scope of simpler, more "rational" processes. Only politics can equate multiple, unlike variables of reason and emotion, of situation and time. Political processes are always, therefore, to some extent mysterious, never wholly subject to analysis. But no one has ever devised anything equally or even similarly harmonious with popular government. Their very complexity attests that they are instruments of popular government.

Popular sentiment varies in effectiveness according to political institutions and processes and the ways in which citizens use them. All governments are at any time the products of the *effective* political sentiments of that time in their respective societies. Democratic societies are those in which the wider popular sentiments have attained their greater effectiveness. No large government in the world surpasses the democratic development of the United States, though the development here has by no means reached its maximum. Even now tens of millions of citizens are powerfully effective. "The" government here is *their* government.

7

It is against a background of some such general, realistic picture of government that administration needs to be considered. Public administration is policy-making. If admission that this is true seems to exalt administration, it must be seen that the emphasis on politics subordinates the administrator, exalts the politicians, and thereby exalts the citizen. Public administration is policy-making. But it is not autonomous, exclusive or isolated policy-making. It is policy-making on a field where mighty forces contend, forces engendered in and by the society. It is policy-making subject to still other and various policy makers. Public administration is one of a number of basic political processes by which this people achieves and controls governance.

INDEX